THE CHICAGO WORLD'S FAIR OF 1893

A PHOTOGRAPHIC RECORD

Photos from the Collections of the
AVERY LIBRARY OF COLUMBIA UNIVERSITY
and the
CHICAGO HISTORICAL SOCIETY

With Text by
STANLEY APPELBAUM

DOVER PUBLICATIONS, INC.
New York

To Bill Engle,
who admires Nikola Tesla

Frontispiece: A corner pavilion of the Agricultural Building.

Published in Canada by General Publishing Company, Ltd., 30 Lesmill Road, Don Mills, Toronto, Ontario.
Published in the United Kingdom by Constable and Company, Ltd.

The Chicago World's Fair of 1893: A Photographic Record is a new work, first published by Dover Publications, Inc., in 1980.

Book design by Carol Belanger Grafton

International Standard Book Number: 0-486-23990-X
Library of Congress Catalog Card Number: 79-54712

Manufactured in the United States of America
Dover Publications, Inc.
180 Varick Street
New York, N.Y. 10014

ACKNOWLEDGMENTS

Thanks are due first and foremost to Dr. Adolf K. Placzek, Avery Librarian at Columbia University, who suggested this book to Dover Publications and made it possible for Dover to photograph directly the 40-odd original platinum-print photographs of the Exposition in the Avery collection.

It is no mere phrase-making when I speak gratefully of the courtesy and helpfulness of Larry A. Viskochil, Curator of the Graphics Collection of the Chicago Historical Society, his assistants Marcia Sommerfeld and Jane Stevens, and all the other staff members with whom it was my pleasure to deal. Nearly 60 of the pictures herein were provided by the Society.

Hayward Cirker, President of Dover, encouraged the project from outset to completion. My editor, James Spero, improved the text in numerous constructive ways.

Michelle Weiss typed the manuscript.

Naturally, any errors are my own and, while fully acknowledging the use I have made of the works listed in the Bibliography, I alone remain responsible for any nuances of opinion that lurk in this basically factual text.

S. A.

NOTE: In October 1979, while the present volume was being set in type, an important exhibition called "The American Renaissance, 1876–1917" opened at The Brooklyn Museum in honor of the centenary of the firm of McKim, Mead and White. Included were original works by numerous artists who were associated with the World's Columbian Exposition. The well-documented catalogue (same title as the exhibition; published by the Museum; with texts by Michael Botwinick, Richard Guy Wilson, Dianne H. Pilgrim and Richard N. Murray) contains the best single statement to date of the ideals and esthetic principles that actuated the artists of this era, with illuminating examples from every branch of the fine and decorative arts. In the terminology of the Brooklyn publication, the architectural epoch inaugurated by the Boston Public Library is "the high or mature period of the American Renaissance."

Another pertinent publication appeared while the present book was being prepared for the press: Reid Badger's *The Great American Fair: The World's Columbian Exposition & American Culture* (Nelson-Hall Publishers, Chicago, 1979). After a brief discussion of the rationale behind Victorian-era world's fairs in general, the heart of the book deals with the preparations for the 1893 fair—the intercity rivalry, organization, financing, promotion and the like—and provides the longest discussion of these matters currently available.

DOVER ARCHITECTURAL SERIES

Adolf K. Placzek
General Editor

PICTURE SOURCES

Avery Architectural and Fine Arts Library, Columbia University in the City of New York (photographs by Charles Dudley Arnold): frontispiece and Figs. 3, 4, 5, 6, 11, 13, 15, 16, 18, 19, 20, 27, 28, 29, 30, 32, 34, 36, 37, 39, 40, 50, 52, 54, 55, 56, 57, 59, 66, 71, 72, 87, 88, 89, 91, 93, 94, 100, 101, 107, 108, 109, 119, 128.

Chicago Historical Society (photographs from the "World's Columbian Exposition, 1893" files): Figs. 1 (halftone; "The Pavilion, Lake Front Pavement. J. P. Craig, Pub."; T14/1888), 2, 7, 8, 12, 14 ("172. Model for Administration Bldg. Jany. 21, 1892"), 23, 24, 25, 26, 31 ("2L. Pediment of Agricultural Building. Copyrighted 1893 by C. D. Arnold"), 33, 35, 38 ("Arch of the Colonnade. Copyrighted 1893 by C. D. Arnold"), 41, 42 (stereograph; "Cross Sectional view of Machinery Building, World's Columbian Exposition. Copyright 1894, by B. W. Kilburn"), 44 ("Harrison, Chicago"), 46, 47, 49, 51, 53, 60, 61 ("Copyrighted 1893 by C. D. Arnold"), 63 ("Copyrighted 1893 by C. D. Arnold"), 65, 69 ("Harrison, Chicago"), 70, 73, 74 ("Copyrighted 1893 by C. D. Arnold"), 75 ("Copyrighted 1893 by C. D. Arnold"), 78 (facsimile typogravure), 79 ("Harrison, Central Music Hall, Chicago"), 81 ("Copyrighted 1893 by C. D. Arnold"), 82, 83 ("Cafe de Marine. Copyrighted 1893 by C. D. Arnold"), 85 ("South Entrance Fisheries Building. Copyrighted 1893 by C. D. Arnold"), 90, 98 ("Turkish Building. Copyrighted 1893 by C. D. Arnold"), 99 ("Harrison, Central Music Hall, Chicago"), 102, 103 ("French Government Building. Copyrighted 1893 by C. D. Arnold"), 104 ("Kaufman & Fabry Co., Photographers"), 105, 106 ("Copyrighted 1893 by C. D. Arnold"), 110 ("Harrison, Chicago"), 111, 112 ("33. Wisconsin State Building. Copyrighted 1893 by C. D. Arnold"), 114 ("The Ste. Maria. Copyrighted 1893 by C. D. Arnold"), 115 ("Harrison, Central Music Hall, Chicago"), 116 ("Forestry Building. Copyrighted 1893 by C. D. Arnold"), 117 ("Harrison, Central Music Hall, Chicago"; Ryerson Collection), 120 ("101. Blarney Castle on the Midway. Copyrighted 1893 by C. D. Arnold"), 121, 123 (stereograph), 124 ("Old Vienna, on the Midway. Copyrighted by C. D. Arnold"), 126, 127.

The map on pages viii and ix is reproduced from *The Century World's Fair Book* (see Bibliography, item 16). Figure 17 is from *Revista de la Exposicion* (Bibliography, item 12). Figure 77 is from *Art and Handicraft in the Woman's Building* (Bibliography, item 10). Figure 118 is from *Das Columbische Weltausstellungs-Album* (Bibliography, item 9).

Official Views of the World's Columbian Exposition (Bibliography, item 1) is the source of Figures 9, 10, 21, 22, 43, 45, 48, 58, 62, 64, 67, 68, 76, 80, 84, 86, 92, 95, 96, 97, 113, 121, 125.

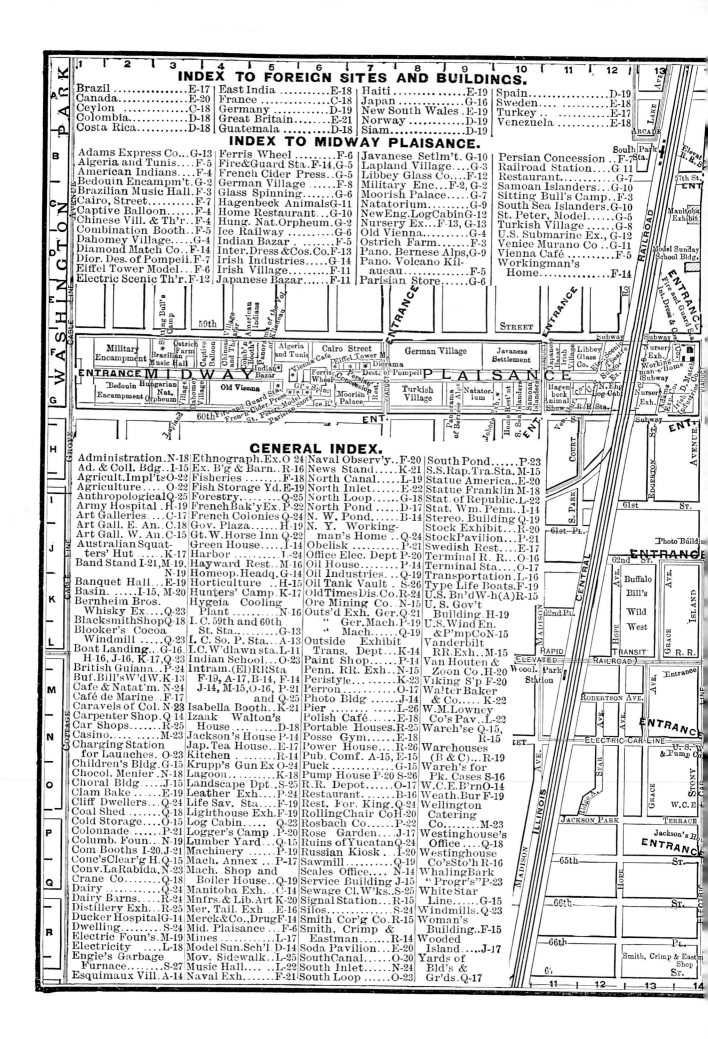

INDEX TO FOREIGN SITES AND BUILDINGS.

INDEX TO MIDWAY PLAISANCE.

GENERAL INDEX.

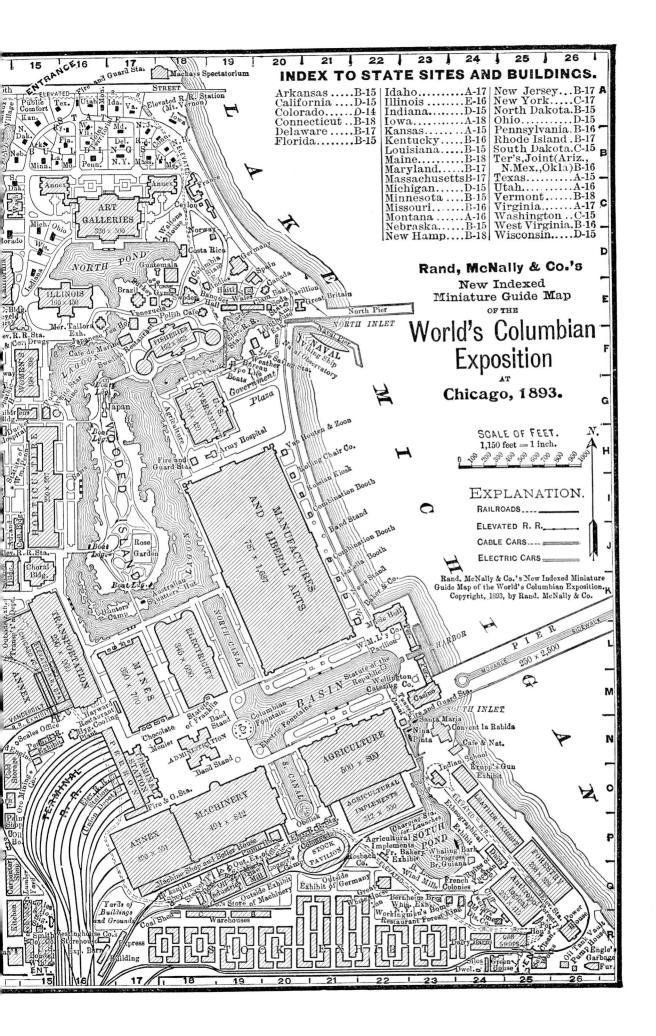

CONTENTS

1

FROM CONCEPTION TO OPENING DAY

Chicago fought hard for the right to host the World's Columbian Exposition, and worked hard to deserve its award. Once the fair looked like a reality, publicity writers attempted to trace to its ultimate source the original idea of holding a large exposition to commemorate the four-hundredth anniversary of Columbus' discovery of America. Conflicting and confused reports, crediting "originators" in several parts of the country, led all the way back to the year of the Philadelphia Centennial. It is clear, however, that in Chicago, businessmen were already seriously contemplating a Columbian fair by the end of 1885.

Large-scale supralocal gatherings had always been important in Chicago's history. In 1847 the national River and Harbor Convention not only helped to create the important canal that eventually linked the city by water to New Orleans; it also introduced many Easterners to Chicago's amazing energy and drive, and attracted new investments and new inhabitants. Nominating conventions of political parties became regularly recurring events after the 1860 Wigwam catapulted the local politician Lincoln to the presidency.

In the specific realm of industrial fairs, Chicago possessed by 1873—less than two full years after the disastrous fire that many believed would write finis to the city's career—an Inter-State Exposition Building in which brief annual early-autumn fairs were held. The publishers of the Inter-State souvenir volume for 1873—three years before the Philadelphia Centennial—called it "the first book of record for any Exposition *ever published in this country.*" Before this building at Michigan and Adams was razed in 1892 to make room for the second (and still current) home of the Art Institute, it had served in many capacities. In 1880 the Republicans nominated Garfield there, and four years later both parties occupied the building, Blaine emerging as the Republicans' choice and Cleveland as the Democrats'. And it was an Inter-State Exposition committee that passed the above-mentioned resolution in 1885 in preparation for a Columbian world's fair.

The fair would naturally have to be backed by Washington. A committee to discuss the project was organized in Congress by the summer of 1886. But it was not until receiving an enormous impetus from the highly successful Exposition Universelle in Paris in 1889 that the American movement became intense and a fierce rivalry developed among the leading cities that wished to give

the fair its local habitation. Washington and Saint Louis were important contenders, but the real struggle was between New York and Chicago. The patrician Eastern city started counting its spare change, and numerous pamphlets were issued to prove that certain undeveloped tracts along Manhattan's rivers, or in Brooklyn, or on Staten Island, were the only logical and sane places to hold a world's fair. It was during this acrimonious period that Chicago received its sobriquet "the windy city." In coining this phrase, Richard Henry Dana of the New York *Sun*, doubtful of Chicago's ability to deliver all it promised, was referring not to the physical blasts from Lake Michigan but to the "hot air" emanating from Chicago boosters.

Most New Yorkers, parochial then as now, really believed that the Chicago of 1889 was a primitive backwater. In actuality, Chicago was already "the second city" in terms of industrial and commercial wealth and power, having long surpassed its older Midwestern rivals Cincinnati and Saint Louis; and in that very year, the inhabitants of 120 square miles of adjacent suburbs and townships voted to become part of Chicago proper, bringing the population within the city limits up to the million mark.

In the cultural and social areas, 1889 saw the founding of Hull House by Jane Addams; and by that year the writers Peter Finley Dunne, Eugene Field and George Ade, along with the cartoonist John McCutcheon and others, had established the intellectual Whitechapel Club. Later than 1889, but still before the fair opened, Theodore Thomas had organized the Chicago Symphony Orchestra, and the Public library, the Newberry Library, the second Art Institute and the second (and still current) University of Chicago had opened their doors, with the Crerar Library soon to follow. In addition, a handful of inventive architects had overtaken and surpassed New York's lead in the development of the tall commercial building, or proto-skyscraper, adding fundamental new esthetic and structural refinements and thereby contributing to the city's tourist attractions.

By mid-August of 1889, a Chicago corporation had been formed (the "World's Exposition of 1892"), which issued five million dollars' worth of bonds; the ten-dollar shares were fully subscribed by April 1890. Chicagoans and others went to study the Paris fair, which not only served as a stimulus (for one thing, it was the first exposition since London's Crystal Palace of 1851 — the ancestor of all modern world's fairs – to end up in the black financially) but also, as will be shown repeatedly in the following pages, was the specific model for innumerable large and small elements of the Chicago fair.

In December 1889, negotiations in Washington were far enough advanced for an Exposition bill to be introduced in the Senate (by Cullom of Illinois). The relentless contest between New York and Chicago was finally decided in the House of Representatives on February 24, 1890, Chicago winning a clear majority only on the eighth ballot. On April 25, President Harrison signed the Exposition bill into law and later in the year issued an official invitation to foreign exhibitors.

The award to Chicago placed most of the detailed planning – as well as almost all of the responsibility, financial and otherwise – in local hands, but also saddled the city with a National Commission of unwieldy proportions which retained the right to determine the overall plan and scope of the fair and to allot exhibition space. This Commission was very vocal during the years of planning and had to be appeased by numerous compromises.

The local Chicago officials were, of course, prominent businessmen and civic leaders. The roster changed several times during the planning period, but when the Exposition finally opened, its President was Harlow N. Higinbotham, a director of Marshall Field and Company, and its First Vice-President was the merchant Ferdinand Wythe Peck, who had conceived of the Auditorium Building (completed by Adler and Sullivan in 1889). Among the Exposition directors at the time of opening were Mayor Carter H. Harrison; traction king and graft-giver supreme Charles T. Yerkes; the outstanding banker Lyman Gage, who had been Chicago's chief Exposition representative in Washington and later became an outstanding proponent of political reform; and the then very young Charles H. Wacker, whose name was destined to be permanently associated with the Chicago urbanistic improvements that can be directly traced to the 1893 fair.

The heads of the Bureau of Photography, to whom many of the pictures in this book are owed, were Charles Dudley Arnold and Harlow N. Higinbotham, Jr. Among the many members of the National Commission whose names are still well known today, let it suffice to mention the Second Vice-President, the San Francisco newspaperman and politician M. H. de Young, who brought an echo of the Chicago fair to his own city in January 1894 (Midwinter Fair) and was a leading organizer of San Francisco's beautiful Panama-Pacific Exposition of 1915.

1890 continued to be a crucial year in the planning of the Chicago fair. Before the end of the year another five-million-dollar bond issue had to be floated, for which it was necessary to obtain state approval in Springfield. It was at this point that the fair acquired its permanent official name: the World's Columbian Exposition. It must also have been roughly around this time that the planners realized the Exposition could not possibly open before 1893. The official reason given for the postponement was that it allowed all other American cities to have their own local celebrations in 1892. This was not to be the last tampering with the calendar.

Also, before 1890 was over, foreign commissioners began to visit statesmen and businessmen in all parts of the world. Eventually, despite foreign merchants' annoyance over the high customs duties imposed by the McKinley Tariff, and such specific grievances as that of China over America's Exclusion Acts, which singled out Chinese as undesirable immigrants, 46 foreign nations participated in the fair, 19 of which erected separate government buildings on the grounds. Another Exposition development of 1890 was the creation of the most high-powered publicity department in history, which ceaselessly churned out literature to familiarize the country and the world with the progress of the fair preparations.

Meanwhile, Chicago was secure in its fair, but precisely where would it be held? What would it look like? Who would build it? Nothing but the best was good enough for the Chicago corporation; in the summer of 1890 Frederick Law Olmsted was hired as landscape architect, and the partners Burnham and Root as chief architects of the buildings, Root being more specifically entrusted with the design, and Burnham with the construction.

Olmsted (1822–1903), one of the most advanced in years of the Exposition planners, was an Easterner; at the time he was summoned, his office was near Boston. World-famous for his work in the New York City area (the design, together with Calvert Vaux, of Central Park and Prospect Park in the 1850s and 60s, and subsequently of Fort Greene, Morningside and Riverside Parks), Olmsted was already associated with the Chicago area as well, having designed the delightful suburb of Riverside, beginning in 1869. In his work for the 1893 fair, Olmsted was ably assisted by the young Henry Sargent Codman.

Burnham and Root were Chicago practitioners. Daniel Hudson Burnham (1846–1912) had come to Chicago in 1855 and, without formal architectural education, had worked for William Le Baron Jenney and others before setting up in partnership with Root in 1873. John Wellborn Root, four years younger than Burnham, had received a degree in engineering in New York in 1869, had worked briefly as a draftsman for James Renwick, architect of Grace Church and Saint Patrick's Cathedral, and had arrived in Chicago in 1871. Together, Burnham and Root had built the structurally innovative Montauk Block in 1881–82 and the grandiose but elegantly refined "Rookery" office block in 1885–86; at the time they were hired for the fair, they were in the midst of constructing the Monadnock Building, which is still famed as the last word in openness, lightness and chaste beauty that could be achieved in that era for a tall commercial building with load-bearing masonry walls. Of the two partners, Root was credited with the larger part of the inventiveness and talent for design, Burnham with more of the business and organizational ability; but this negative evaluation of Burnham has been colored by the highly personal reminiscences of the eccentric geniuses Louis Sullivan and Frank Lloyd Wright.

At this early planning stage, a dual site was envisioned for the fair, with the majority of the buildings to be located in the Jackson Park area and a few on the lakefront on land now part of Grant Park. In December 1890, Root drew a very informal plan on brown paper, showing the principal distribution of landscape elements (Basin, Canals, Lagoon with Island) and of main building sites for the southern (Jackson Park) location; this plan remained definitive in most essentials. In the same month, Burnham submitted an all-important memorandum to the Exposition corporation, in which he pointed out that the construction of the buildings could be assigned either to a single architect or to a number of architects, who might win first place in either an open or an invited competition for the individual buildings, or might be directly selected by Exposition authorities. Selection of several architects, championed by Burnham for the sake of expediency, uniform appearance of buildings and other considerations, won the day, and Burnham was granted ultimate responsibility for the choices.

After Burnham held consultations in the East, the New York firm of McKim, Mead and White was given the assignment for the Agricultural Building; George B. Post of New York received the contract for the Manufactures Building; Richard M. Hunt of New York, that for the Administration Building; Peabody and Stearns of Boston, that for Machinery Hall; Charles B. Atwood of Boston and New York, that for the Palace of Fine Arts. The Mining, Transportation, Horticultural and Fisheries Buildings were reserved for Chicagoans. The Electricity Building was also apparently a gain for the West, being granted to the Kansas City firm of Van Brunt and Howe; but these men were Easterners, too, and Van Brunt proved to be the most articulate spokesman of the new academic style that caused the fair to be known as the White City.

This decision of Burnham's and the consequent influx of Eastern architects, accompanied by the sculptors and muralists who had collaborated with them in the past, led to a controversy that is far from being settled today, and that has done more than anything else to keep the Exposition alive in people's memories.

The planners from East and West exchanged ideas frequently during the winter of 1890–91, often while enjoying the generous fare of Chicago's leading restaurateurs. There was much friendly give-and-take with a view to the overriding architectural ideals of the fair (uniform cornice height, standardized bay modules, regulated dome height, etc.). The preeminent New York sculptor Augustus Saint-Gaudens, who had been offered $15,000 to supervise all Exposition sculpture but had modestly agreed merely "to indicate the general scheme" for $3,000, is reported to have called one of these gatherings of the planners the greatest meeting of artistic minds since the Renaissance.* The strain of the congenial get-togethers apparently overtaxed the strength of the highly respected architect Root, who died of pneumonia on January 15, 1891. This unfortunate event provided the

Exposition with a martyr, and allowed both sides in the architectural dispute to claim ever after, largely with insufficient foundation, that Root, the consummate artist, would never have countenanced this or that decision, that everything would have been altered for the good if he had lived, and so on. Root's death left Burnham in sole charge of design and construction, with the title of Director of Works.

By February 1891 a firm decision was reached to have a single site for the fair, Jackson Park. Considerations of transit were particularly vital in making this decision. Up to that period in Chicago's history, the South Side led in public transportation; moreover, the powerful Illinois Central Railroad lobbied strongly for the southern site. Land had been set aside for a park along the lake between 55th and 67th Streets as early as 1870; Olmsted pointed out in an 1893 paper that — as in the case of the Manhattan sites of Central, Morningside, Riverside, Mount Morris and Tompkins Square Parks, and of such European park sites as Battersea and the Tuileries — the Jackson Park site had originally been set aside for public use because it was considered unfavorable for profitable construction.

Before the Exposition preparations, the northernmost part of Jackson Park had already been developed, and there was a "French château"-style service building at the northeastern corner known as the Pavilion (see Fig. 1); this building was to be revamped for the fair, as will appear later. Nevertheless, Olmsted described the Jackson Park site as it appeared in 1890 as "the least parklike ground within miles of the city." It consisted of marshy flats covered with reeds and scrub vegetation, and the landscaping activity that made it essentially the Jackson Park of today was a herculean effort.

As work on the fair progressed, many architectural and landscaping ideas were given up. For instance, where the Peristyle eventually rose, a Venetian Village was to have stood. What this would have meant to the very academic Court of Honor is difficult to imagine. Yet through a sort of inertia, the Venetian scheme still largely colored the finished fair, with its prominent canals and ubiquitous gondolas.

Work on the Mining and Transportation Buildings was begun by July 1891. The unfinished Horticulture greenhouse served as a studio for the designers and decorators. Delightful contemporary magazine accounts tell of inspiriting concerts that were arranged for the artists by Theodore Thomas, and of their communal lunches, from which they were whisked to their respective working areas by electric launches.

By February 1892 there was enough standing on the grounds to impress a large group of Congressmen who had been invited to inspect the site. More money was urgently needed from the federal government. Eventually, a Columbian 50-cent piece was coined by the Treasury and, together with several constricting stipulations, two and a half million dollars' worth of the coins was presented to the Exposition corporation, who sold them as souvenirs at a total of about twice their face value. The very first half-dollar of the issue was purchased for

*Saint-Gaudens was no stranger to Chicago, having already created the magnificent *Lincoln* in Lincoln Park, with an architectural setting by his longtime collaborator in this field, McKim's partner Stanford White. Saint-Gaudens would later provide *General Logan* for Grant Park (horse by A. Phimister Proctor).

1. The pavilion in the northeast corner of Jackson Park, 1888. 2. A group of Exposition planners. Left to right: Daniel H. Burnham, Director of Works; George B. Post, architect of Manufactures; M. B. Pickett, Secretary of Works; Henry Van Brunt, co-architect of Electricity; Francis D. Millet, Director of Decoration; Maitland Armstrong; Col. Edmund Rice, Commandant of the Columbian Guard; Augustus Saint-Gaudens, adviser on sculpture; Henry Sargent Codman, landscape architect; George W. Maynard, muralist for Agriculture; Charles F. McKim, architect of Agriculture; Ernest R. Graham, Assistant Director of Works; and Dion Geraldine, general supervisor of construction.

$10,000 by the Remington Typewriter Company, which displayed the coin in its exhibit inside the Manufactures Building.

The public was allowed onto the grounds during construction. So popular a pastime did this become that even after free passes had been abolished, even after admission to the unfinished fair had been raised from 25 to 50 cents, the workmen were constantly hampered by up to 5,000 gawkers at a time.

Generally speaking, the major buildings were largely iron and timber sheds, resembling the traditional train shed in construction. The cladding, or outer surfacing of the buildings—and the varying architectural "styles" adopted affected the surface only—was largely executed in staff, a lightweight but firm and reasonably durable mixture of plaster, cement and jute fibers. Staff, invented in France in the 1860s or 70s, had already been extensively employed in European fairs. Apparently in an effort to mask the many French borrowings in the Chicago Exposition, some official writers gave it out that the builders had adopted the material from South America, where it had been used for a century; but the *Official Guide* to the fair admitted the French origin of staff (which was the chief material of the fair statuary as well), and most of the staff workers in Chicago were French or Belgian.

The color of the main buildings was still a matter of lively discussion in May 1892, at which time some of the structures later noted for their serene whiteness were still slated for more polychromatic treatment. Reports vary on just when the Englishman William Pretyman (or Prettyman), a friend of the regretted Root, stepped down as Director of Decoration and was replaced by the Eastern painter Francis D. Millet, who taught at the Art Institute of Chicago; but by December of 1892 Millet was proclaiming in print that white was the only suitable color for the Court of Honor. Many writers see the necessity for speed as a major influence on the decision that created the White City. The white paint was applied by compressed-air squirt guns, which were used here for the first time on a major project.

The buildings were far from being finished when Dedication Day rolled around, even though the day itself had been delayed. October 12, the date of Columbus' discovery, had naturally been selected initially, but a change was made to October 26. It was explained that the later day was the "correct date of the discovery according to the New-Style calendar." Thousands of people were crammed into the Manufactures Building to hear Vice-President Levi Morton (President Harrison was prevented from coming by his wife's fatal illness) and such orators of national repute as Henry Watterson of Louisville and Chauncey M. Depew of New York City. The august actress Sarah Cowell LeMoyne read portions of the *Columbian Ode* that had been penned by Harriet Monroe, devoted sister-in-law of the architect Root and later editor of the world-renowned magazine *Poetry;* choral sections of the *Ode* had been set to music by the eminent George W. Chadwick.

The winter of 1892–93 was extremely severe and made construction work difficult and dangerous. (The fair was perilous to workmen in general; it is said that in 1891 alone there were 700 accidents, 18 of them fatal.) On January 13, 1893, nearly two years to the day after the death of Root, Olmsted's gifted young assistant Codman succumbed to illness.

On March 6, 1893, Burnham was honored with a public dinner, said to be the first tendered to an artist in the United States. On April 27, an international naval review was held in New York harbor as part of the Exposition celebrations. As opening day, May 1, approached and major construction finally ended, a ban on coal as an energy source was enacted on the fairgrounds, so that the White City could remain white for the duration of the Exposition (in contrast with Chicago itself, which was soon dubbed the Gray City).

The fair now being poised to open, a few statistics are in order. Including the ⅞-mile-long amusement area along the Midway Plaisance, the broad thoroughfare that connects Jackson and Washington Parks and is bordered on the north by the University of Chicago, the area of the Exposition was 633 acres (as compared to 160 for Paris 1889), far and away the largest up to that time. Added to the dozen or so major buildings and their dependencies, and to the 19 foreign-government and 38 state-government buildings, the service structures and individual exhibitors' pavilions (not countenanced in the original plan, and admitted to Olmsted's regret) brought the total of separate buildings to about 200. It was estimated that to see everything in the fair once quickly, a visitor would need about three weeks and would have to walk over 150 miles.

Transportation from the heart of the city cost a nickel by streetcar or municipal elevated railway (the latter, powered by steam, was extended to its present 63rd Street terminus specially for the fair); 20 cents for a round trip on the Illinois Central's "cattle cars"; 25 cents for a round trip by whaleback steamboat from the foot of Van Buren Street.

Transportation on the fairgrounds included an elevated electric Intramural Railway that was a pioneer in the third-rail method of supplying power; this ran from the South Pond to the North Inlet, with several stations, and cost 20 cents for a ride of any distance. On the waterways, a round-trip gondola ride cost 50 cents, which was also the price for an hour's trip by electric launch. Steam launches, which ran out into the lake for part of their course, cost a quarter. A controversial and ultimately financially unsuccessful type of conveyance (too undemocratic in that age of rugged individualism?) was the rolling chair, which cost 40 cents an hour or $6.00 a day with guide, or $3.50 a day without guide (there had been rolling chairs at Paris in 1889). The chairs were pushed by college students, so many of whom were theology majors that the conveyances came to be known as "gospel chariots." In general, there were many complaints that the in-fair transportation was insufficient.

Folding camp chairs could be rented at 10 cents a day

(25 cents deposit); this concession* had made such a shrewd deal that relatively little public seating was available on the grounds. This example is typical of the important role the concessions eventually assumed. But then, without them, and principally the amusement concessions, the fair would have been a financial failure, as will be seen.

There was a large number of restaurants, cafés, teahouses, lunch counters and refreshment stands on the grounds for those who eat their way through shows. The sanitation and the general maintenance were highly praised and held up as a model for real cities to follow. The Exposition police force, the semimilitary Columbian Guard, though called "tin soldiers" by some, performed useful services on many occasions. Toilets were plentiful for that day and age, and water could be had free at many locations; mineral water cost splurgers a penny. Alcohol could be obtained only at tables in restaurants.

Adult admission to the fairgrounds was 50 cents, very high at the time but surely well worth it. Children under

*Perhaps the same company that hired out the rolling chairs.

12 could get in for 25 cents, and for only 10 cents during one week in October. Under six, they were admitted free. There were very few exhibits on the main (nonamusement) part of the grounds for which an additional charge was made. On the Midway Plaisance (the name Midway was later adopted by countless amusement lanes in fairs and carnivals), the attractions varied in price, but it was estimated that a strong-willed person could see each and every one for a total of $13.05. One fee that caused irritation was the two-dollar-a-day license for private cameras—and no tripods allowed. Naturally the Bureau of Photography wished to dispose of its own product.

Opening day, May 1, 1893, finally arrived. Grover Cleveland, President once more after the unsavory Harrison administration, made a speech in front of the Administration Building and pressed a button, turning on electric lights and motors everywhere. The excited crowd surged forward. Several women fainted in the crush. Jane Addams' purse was snatched. The Exposition was on.

2

THE ARCHITECTURAL PROGRAM

A somewhat disappointed foreign observer at the World's Columbian Exposition remarked that world's fairs were then following one another with such speed that it was ungenerous to expect new scientific wonders at each one; and it is true that, despite considerable evidence in Chicago of technological progress, there was no real "breakthrough" invention to be seen in a fairly perfected state, such as the telephone and phonograph had been in the past.*There is no doubt, and it was widely repeated at the time, that the chief marvel of the Exposition was its architecture—to the extent that a leading exhibitors' organization officially complained that the Exposition was not an industrial fair at all, but an architectural show!

As an architectural show, the Exposition was extraordinarily successful, for the White City style, which had just won its titles of nobility in the East but was a novelty to the rest of the nation, proved so attractive that its influence made itself immediately felt from coast to coast, and lasted for decades.

As the fashionable mode, it was axiomatically admired in architectural writing up to about 1925, when the appeal of more modernistic stirrings in Europe and the stinging criticism of the aging Louis Sullivan and his disciple Claude Bragdon ushered in the theory of the "lost cause." According to this view of events, which went practically unchallenged until 1950 and still has its adherents today, the World's Columbian Exposition singlehandedly killed architecture in the United States; that is, it brought to a sudden end those tendencies, chiefly localized in Chicago, which were producing relatively unadorned commercial buildings framed in steel with curtain walls, in which outer appearance was nearly a pure expression of the structural elements. That style (which, in this teleological theory, is the only true one, toward which all rightminded architects must strive) then had to be reimported from Europe about 1930.

According to Sullivan and those who repeated his ingenious and infectiously sardonic formulations, Burnham sold out his Chicago colleagues when he hired the New York clique. Sullivan's famous pronunciamento that the "damage wrought by the World's Fair will last for half a century from its date, if not longer" takes on an awesomely prophetic weight when those who quote it fail to realize or fail to acknowledge that it was published fully 31 years after the Exposition. Likewise, whether Sullivan

*Although in *The Great American Fair* Badger correctly points out the importance in 1893 of the electric light bulb and alternating current.

and Bragdon were right or wrong esthetically, they were at least disingenuous when they called the White City ornamental motifs old and hackneyed. The motifs were most certainly new to the eyes of millions accustomed to prevailing Gothic Revival, Queen Anne, Romanesque and vernacular styles.

Since 1950 the good side of the White City has been increasingly emphasized, and the Beaux-Arts tradition that suffused the new academic style has received fresh appreciation. For one thing, it has been pointed out that the "Chicago School" of architecture did not vanish with the fair; that, in fact, some of the most honored achievements of the first Chicago generation (Reliance Building; Carson, Pirie, Scott store; and others) came after the fair; that a second generation, the "Prairie School," created many fine buildings; and that other factors, such as an increasing interest in the designing of residences, contributed to the falling off of creative commercial building in Chicago.

For another thing, careful critics have shown that even in its heyday, the Chicago commercial style proceeded by fits and starts and manifested many anomalies in structural methods and ornamentation. For example, after Root's death he was invoked as a patron saint by the stark-functionalists, but of his last two completed designs, the Woman's Temple (for the Women's Christian Temperance Union) was Romanesque and Gothic in outer style and the Masonic Temple used Venetian and Tudor design elements. On the other hand, in the very year of the fair, Frank Lloyd Wright, who had worked with Sullivan and was later a vocal opponent of the White City, submitted a thoroughly academic design for a museum and library in Milwaukee.

Burnham's reputation has also been salvaged recently, and he is now less often looked down upon as a personally untalented exploiter of others. It has been shown that the initial selection of Burnham and Root as chiefs of the Exposition architecture, when Richard Morris Hunt was a strong contender, signified a tremendous victory for Chicago, and not a "sellout"; that Burnham had to satisfy the National Commission in his choice of individual architects; that the fair was *in* Chicago, but a national effort (in fact, had to appeal to world visitors, too); that the selection of the Eastern men was in the interests of professionalism, rationality, harmony and efficiency.

It has also been argued that the Chicago architects at the Exposition were in actuality not "punished" by receiving "unglamorous" assignments; that, in fact, the idea for

3. Roman classicism at the Exposition: a corner of the Agricultural Building.

a separate Transportation Building (the structure designed by Sullivan) came from Sullivan himself.

Last but not least, the White City style would never have supplanted older traditions so swiftly and decidedly if the public had not been psychologically ready for it at the time.

True as all this is, it is still possible to sympathize with the later resentment of the Chicagoans. It cannot be denied that, at Burnham's invitation, the "small white cloud" from the East descended on the Western metropolis with a vengeance, swarms of painters and sculptors following in the wake of the architects.

Richard Morris Hunt (1827–1895), designer of the fair's Administration Building,* was the dean of his profession and President of the American Institute of Architects (of which he was cofounder) when invited to Chicago. After long study at the Ecole des Beaux-Arts in Paris, he had assisted Hector-Martin Lefuel in designing the 1854–55 additions to the Louvre, the seminal building of the Second Empire style. Back in the United States, he had assisted Thomas Ustick Walter on the Capitol dome in Washington. Settling in New York, he had introduced that city to successive styles of French classic architecture in such buildings as the Stuyvesant Apartments (as early as 1869–70) and the Lenox Library. His numerous prestigious assignments had included the base of the

* A small model of the building forms part of Daniel Chester French's memorial sculpture for Hunt in New York, opposite the Frick Collection on Fifth Avenue.

Statue of Liberty and the Vanderbilt mausoleum on Staten Island (for which Olmsted did the landscaping). It should not be forgotten that it was also Hunt who had designed the nine-story *New York Tribune* building, considered by many to be the first skyscraper. In Chicago, Hunt had built a house for Marshall Field.

The Agricultural Building at the fair (not to mention a number of less official structures) was the work of the bustling New York firm of McKim, Mead and White, of which Charles Follen McKim (1847–1909) was head and Stanford White (1853–1906) chief designer. McKim studied architecture at the Beaux-Arts from 1867 to 1870 and became assistant to Henry Hobson Richardson in 1872. He joined forces with William Rutherford Mead in 1877. White (another Richardson alumnus, having been his chief assistant on Trinity Church in Boston) came into the firm in 1879 and achieved partnership two years later. McKim, Mead and White first became famous for their residences, moving from sophisticated examples of the "shingle style" to a Neocolonial approach. After they became associated with public buildings, they chalked up a remarkable list that eventually included the Villard Houses, the second (and greatest) Madison Square Garden, Columbia University and Pennsylvania Station (all in New York) and dozens of other "plums" in their headquarters city and elsewhere. Most significant with regard to the Exposition was the Boston Public Library, begun just a few years previously. Viewed in Boston, too, as pushy outsiders, the firm, against much opposition

4. Grecian classicism at the Exposition: Atwood's Palace of Fine Arts.

that was gradually won over, produced in the Library *the* showcase building for Beaux-Arts academicism in America (with D. C. French and Augustus Saint-Gaudens as sculptural decorators and a pleiad of major muralists).

George B. Post (1837–1913), who designed the Manufactures Building, was a pupil of R. M. Hunt (whom he succeeded as President of the American Institute of Architects), becoming an independent architect in New York in 1860. Deeply concerned with engineering and technology, Post was among the first to introduce elevators and central heating in his office buildings. His ten-story Western Union Building of 1873–75, one of the first skyscrapers, was in the Second Empire style; his 1878 Long Island Historical Society building in Brooklyn Heights remains a gem of the Queen Anne style; his 1884 Produce Exchange was built around an iron skeleton; and he flirted with the French Renaissance in his 1889–90 building for Pulitzer's *World*. Assignments after the Exposition included the north campus of the College of the City of New York in 1905.

The Boston firm of Peabody and Stearns, successors to Richardson's business in that city, executed Machinery Hall, the Colonnade and the Obelisk at the fair. Robert Swain Peabody (1845–1917) studied in Paris and was a pupil of Henry Van Brunt. The firm has one extant New York City building to its credit, the immediately post-fair (1894) J. J. Emery House, now occupied by Indonesia's mission to the UN.

It was McKim who brought Charles B. Atwood

(1849–1895) to Chicago as an Exposition designer (Palace of Fine Arts and other buildings). Atwood stayed on for the few years that remained to him, replacing Root as chief designer in Burnham's office. In Chicago he completed the plans for the Reliance Building, which has been called epoch-making and prophetic for its functionalist contours and its "skin" of terra-cotta. Earlier, Atwood had worked for Van Brunt and had taught architecture in Boston and at Columbia.

It is usually stated that the ten major fair buildings were divided half and half between East and West, but the Electricity Building is an anomaly. Of the Kansas City firm of Van Brunt and Howe, Frank Maynard Howe (1849–1909), born in Massachusetts and trained in Boston, was a pupil of Van Brunt, opening the Western branch of his teacher's business in 1885; and Henry Van Brunt himself (1832–1903), though in Kansas City since 1887, was a dyed-in-the-wool Bostonian who proudly proclaimed himself as the pupil of R. M. Hunt and the mentor of Howe, Peabody and Stearns. Van Brunt had put up public buildings all over the United States; he succeeded Post as President of the American Institute of Architects. A highly literate man who had translated Viollet-le-Duc's *Discourses on Architecture*, Van Brunt published articles on the Exposition that form the most thorough and conscious statement of the Easterners' ideals.

Since Hunt had also taught Post, and since Atwood, McKim and White (the latter two being pupils of

Richardson) had received comparable training and influences, it is readily seen that the White City architects, with their personal entourage of sculptors and painters, comprised a formidable clique. Many of them had in common a Parisian period of training in their respective fields, usually at the Ecole des Beaux-Arts. (Most of the Chicago architects had a strong engineering background and basically only "on-the-job" training in architecture.)

Various ways have been suggested by architectural historians for viewing the affiliations and the oppositions among late nineteenth-century American practitioners. One approach is to contrast Beaux-Arts trainees with functional-minded engineers. This contrast is also employed by French historians of the French architectural trends of the period. In American terms, it is tantamount to an opposition between Hunt together with Richardson on one hand, and on the other, Chicago's engineering genius William Le Baron Jenney (architect of the Fair's Horticultural Building), who had studied at the Ecole Polytechnique rather than the Beaux-Arts and through whose office Burnham, Sullivan, Holabird and Roche had passed.

Another school of thought sets at odds the two great Beaux-Arts graduates Hunt and Richardson, contrasting the former's classic elegance with the latter's powerful structural sense. A third view is that everything in the American 1890s was due to the one giant Richardson, who combined English picturesque ideals with his Beaux-Arts traditions, and whose mantle was sliced in two, McKim inheriting his love of clarity and order, and Sullivan continuing his structural advances.

In many of these discussions, the notion of what the Ecole des Beaux-Arts really stood for often becomes clouded. Even when one accepts the current, more sympathetic view of Beaux-Arts, it is still undeniable that the school preached the need to clad the exterior of a building in historic styles, sometimes more pure, sometimes disconcertingly eclectic, with a marked preference for styles of antiquity and the Renaissance. But although today's architects may no longer agree with the Beaux-Arts philosophy that there are "laws" of composition, more respect is being paid to the external and internal arrangement of Beaux-Arts buildings, with their stable harmony dependent on symmetrical or balanced masses; their strong axes; the clarity of their boundaries at ground level, cornice level and sides; their gradual modulations and transitions from one element to another; and the ambitious engineering that lay behind their monumentality and ceremonial planning.*

Not enough attention has been paid by historians to the Beaux-Arts principle that the appearance of a building

*The discussion of the Beaux-Arts style here owes a great deal to the pages on the subject in the book by Jordy cited as item 54 in the Bibliography.

5. "Town planning" at the Exposition. A well thought-out short prospect: general view of the South Canal. Left to right: Agricultural Building, Colonnade with Obelisk in front of it, Machinery Hall, Columbian Fountain. A. Phimister Proctor was the sculptor of the elk on the bridge.

6. "Town planning" at the Exposition. A carefully composed long prospect: the west end of the Basin. Seen from the left: an electric fountain, Administration Building, Columbian Fountain, Electricity Building, North Canal with the dome of the Illinois Building in the distance, Manufactures Building.

should match the character of the assignment. The World's Columbian Exposition architects did not suddenly and definitively abandon Gothic Revival and other styles, as careless writers have suggested. For instance, George B. Post's Gothic design for City College was done long after the fair, but within a stylistic tradition of Gothic for colleges. Atwood's Palace of Fine Arts was considered the acme of classicism at the fair but, as the Exposition's Designer-in-Chief after Root's death, he also designed a number of secondary buildings that were quite different in style. During the tour of the fairgrounds in the following three chapters, several other examples will be noted.

The Beaux-Arts method of construction was also an extremely rational one. It has been said that buildings of the White City type are "more spacious, easier to build, and more effectively illuminated" than their Gothic and Romanesque predecessors; that the classic norm is the natural result of rationalizing the approaches to mass and space. These methods were also particularly suitable to the then-emerging corporate practice in the organization of architectural studios, of which Burnham's, both the regular one in the heart of Chicago and the temporary one on the fairgrounds, were important pioneering examples.*

So, then, the White City (it should be recalled that only the Court of Honor buildings and the Palace of Fine Arts really qualify for this designation) was a product of

*Of course, the Beaux-Arts had its opponents in nineteenth-century France as well. Frantz Jourdain, later to design the steel-frame, ceramic-clad Samaritaine department store in Paris, wrote about the majority of the 1889 fair buildings in terms of disgust that curiously anticipate Louis Sullivan's outbursts by 36 years: "The training at the Ecole des Beaux-Arts, with its ill-digested decisions, its narrow exclusiveness and its prehistoric pedagogy, has perhaps done more harm to our country than any epidemic, invasion or other cataclysm; its influence has been particularly pernicious in architecture."

Beaux-Arts training, and was classical and Renaissance in style. But within its general classicism, it had a particularly strong tinge of Roman Empire styling in its triumphal arches, arcades, domes, applications of architectural sculpture and painted panels, and many other features. This Romanism, which was to remain an essential element of the White City style as it spread through the country, seems to have been a new twist in the work of McKim and his colleagues, barely adumbrated earlier and not strongly present in the Boston Public Library, the test piece of the academic reaction back East. No architectural historian has yet explained in detail just why this Romanism was able to burst forth suddenly at the Exposition.

Of course, Roman styling (modified at the fair by a lingering Second Empire insistence on central and corner pavilions) had precedents in American architectural history. The Jeffersonian style had been largely Roman via Palladio; is it merely idle to compare the symmetrical layout of the Court of Honor, the octagonal-domed Administration at its head, with the main layout of the

University of Virginia and its corresponding library rotunda? (As will be seen, there was also more recent French inspiration for the Court of Honor.) Many government buildings in early nineteenth-century Washington were "Roman" too.* Moreover, the permanent "Roman" dome of the Capitol (on which R. M. Hunt worked) arose during the 1860s, at the height of the Second Empire craze; and the imitation of the dome of the national Capitol on numerous state capitols (another example of style dictated by specific assignment) had kept a classical flame flickering through all of the intervening period.

Still, the White City struck most viewers as something bold and new—and desirably new, not freakish. It seemed to suit the temper of the country, which was actively turning from the conquest of its own territory to imperial conquests overseas (Hawaii was almost annexed in the year of the Exposition). It seemed to suit the psy-

*Like the 1893 fair, Washington had been a planned city for which distinguished architects (such as Bulfinch) had been called in from other parts of the country.

chological needs of the newest group of millionaires, who tended to be suave financiers rather than lusty self-made men. Its Romanism was that of the Empire, not that of the Republic, as Jefferson's had been. Some writers have said that the neat and dainty whiteness of the Exposition appealed especially to the millionaires' ladies; others have seen the whiteness as a kind of nostalgia for the prevalent stone cladding of Paris. Henry-Russell Hitchcock considers the classicism of the fair not as an enslavement to European traditions, but as a declaration of independence from the English principles that had dominated Richardson's production and the Brown Decades!

Was the enormous success of the Exposition architecture as much of a surprise to its builders as they claimed? Van Brunt officially asked foreign critics to judge America's recent architecture by the actual examples they would find in her cities; the fair, he announced, would be "an unsubstantial pageant." The "vast covered inclosures" would be "adjusted to . . . the most effective arrangement of the materials [exhibited]" and "faced with a decorative mask . . . as the Romans of the Empire clothed their rough structures of cement and brick with magnificent architectural veneers of marbles, bronze and sculpture." The buildings would not "express actual structure [like Paxton's Crystal Palace]" but would "rather serve as architectural screens."* It is hard to believe that Van Brunt was perfectly honest when he went on to say: "It is not desired or expected that this display, however successful it may prove to be in execution, should make a new revival or a new school." After all, in the same 1892 article, as in a later one, he insisted that the fair's Roman classic harmony would be "on trial before the world" as a sorely needed corrective to the deplorable national tendency to experiment in an "impure and unhealthy vernacular."† That he included the whole "Chicago School" in the latter category becomes evident from other ultra-

*Yet the Exposition facades and openings were more closely expressive of interior axes, naves, and upper stories than many a "picturesque" building of the Brown Decades, in which facade entrances could be as false as the fronts on a Western boomtown main street.

†Another expression of Van Brunt's was "outworn vernacular architecture, with all its offensive and ungoverned crudities of detail."

Brahmin remarks about the barbarism that still needed to be dispelled in the benighted West.

A public-relations concern with instruction also emerges from a December 1892 article by Francis D. Millet, the Director of Decoration: "A few short months ago there was in this country but a very limited number of full-sized reproductions of any of the notable details of ancient architecture. . . . Now the whole range of details, from the beautiful Ionic capitals of the Temple of Minerva Polias to the mouldings of the Arch of Titus, are practically at the command of any architect and student."

All disclaimers and high-minded aims set aside, the "expert salesmanship" recalled by Sullivan must have occupied much of the time of the Exposition architects in the year of the fair and the years just before and after.

There was one architectural achievement at the fair, however, that has received practically universal acclaim from that day to this: its town-planning aspect. In refreshing contrast to the wild growth of actual cities in the late nineteenth century, the main lines of the Exposition layout offered the first widely publicized, well-planned ensemble of public buildings within the memory of living Americans, and the first anywhere since Haussmann had reorganized the heart of Paris and Vienna's "ring" system had been created. The Exposition has been called a "restoration of the principle of coordination"; Van Brunt wanted it to demonstrate that "order is heaven's first law."

After the fair, Burnham became increasingly involved in town planning, and participated in new plans for Washington (1902, with McKim and F. L. Olmsted, Jr.), Manila (1905) and San Francisco (1906). The culmination of these efforts, and Burnham's greatest boon to his fellow citizens, was his heroic and far-sighted Chicago Plan of 1907–09, many aspects of which have subsequently been implemented (Michigan Avenue Bridge, Wacker Drive and much more). In turn, the Chicago Plan has been a seminal document for countless civic centers, traffic systems and urban improvements around the globe. And it is no exaggeration to trace it directly back to the World's Columbian Exposition.

THE COURT OF HONOR
AND ITS BUILDINGS

Any tour of the World's Columbian Exposition should begin in the southern part of the grounds with the Court of Honor, the real White City. The Court consisted of a number of the noblest buildings, the porticos and arcades of which—though remaining inside the building lines—formed a continuous stoa around a Basin 350 feet wide and 1,100 feet long. The Basin had a northeast-southwest orientation, but the standard mild fiction of calling it east-west is followed here.

As originally planned, the principal access to the Exposition was to have been through the Terminal Station (Figs. 7–9), from which visitors would have passed through or around the Administration Building into the Basin area. The crucial refusal of the Illinois Central to participate in this joint railway approach thwarted the plan, and the $400,000 station, designed by Atwood in a relatively pure Roman-bath style (it was 458 feet long, 162 feet wide and 84 feet high), remained relatively unused and unnoticed, although one writer called it the "foremost among the Exposition structures which are not halls of exhibitions."*

Richard Morris Hunt's Administration Building (Figs. 10–15) presided over the west end of the Basin. (Foreign visitors saw in the Basin-area arrangement a clear reminiscence of the layout of the main buildings of the Paris 1889 fair on the Champ de Mars, with the Administration Building occupying the position of the Eiffel Tower.) Generally in a "French Renaissance" style, the Administration Building cost $493,901 and covered an area of 55,000 square feet. Its four Doric corner pavilons, each 84 feet square, were 65 feet high and had window bays about 20 feet wide. This cornice height and bay width were standard, with slight variations, for the Court of Honor. Roofs and domes were allowed to loom above this, especially the dome of Administration,† which was intended to be a landmark from all points of the Exposi-

tion. Thus, the second stage of the building, continuing the central rotunda and ringed with an open Ionic colonnade, was as high as the first; and finally the dome, 120 feet in diameter, rose to a height of 250 feet above the ground. Inside the rotunda, a clear space led up to an inner dome (with a Pantheon-like "eye") 190 feet high; this was decorated with murals by William de Leftwich Dodge, who, 26 when the fair opened, was the youngest of the painters commissioned to decorate the Exposition.

The exterior of the building was dotted with enormous sculptural groups by Austrian-born Karl Bitter, then a relatively unknown protégé of Hunt's, but later to be director of sculpture at the Buffalo (1901) and Saint Louis (1904) fairs, and familiar to New Yorkers for such works as the statue on the Pulitzer Fountain in Manhattan's Grand Army Plaza. An accident to one of Bitter's Administration sculptures early in the fair led to the closing of the promenade at the base of the dome. Outside the west entrance stood a huge statue of Columbus by Mary Lawrence, a pupil of Augustus Saint-Gaudens (it had been commenced by his brother Louis).

At an early planning stage, Administration was to have been the center of all Exposition services, but these were eventually dispersed. As it turned out, one of its pavilions housed the National Commission along with telegraph and messenger services; another, the Exposition executives and customs officials; another, the Exposition newspaper and other information and publicity departments; another, a bank, an express office, the Columbian Guards station and the bureau of foreign affairs.

No building in the Court of Honor was without some touches of color here or there, although white predominated. Thus, the walls behind Administration's second-stage colonnade were painted a dull red, and its dome was gilded and otherwise decorated.

In the Basin to the left and right of Administration were two electric fountains (another feature borrowed from Paris 1889 and traceable to a London exposition of 1884). Rather homely by day, they were festive with colored lights at night. They spurted 150 feet high, thus surpassing the electric fountains that traction magnate Yerkes had already donated to Chicago's Lincoln Park.

But the greatest Exposition fountain of them all, praised with an extravagance that is disconcerting today, stood in the Basin directly in front of Administration (Fig. 16). It was the work of a young pupil of Saint-Gaudens, the Brooklyn-born Frederick William MacMonnies,

---

*Since the tour will not return to this corner of the grounds, this is the place in which to mention the Cold Storage Building, which appears prominently in Fig. 7. This "greatest refrigerator on earth" (130 by 255 feet), ice-maker to the Exposition, with a skating rink on an upper story, was built in a Romanesque style by another Chicago Burnham, Franklin P. It was a concession of the Hercules Iron Works. Fire, a constant threat to the fair buildings, struck first at Cold Storage, on July 10, 1893, when negligently exposed wooden elements of its smokestack ignited. Seventeen firemen were killed when the tower collapsed with them.

†For convenience, and following sources contemporary with the fair, we shall use short forms for many building names after their first introduction: Administration, Agriculture, Machinery, Mining, Electricity, Manufactures, Transportation, Horticulture, Fisheries, Fine Arts and so on.

7

8

7. At the right, the tracks leading to the Terminal Station, with the Administration dome looming above the Station. At the left, the Cold Storage Building in the foreground, with the Transportation annex and building behind it. **8.** A head-on view of the Terminal Station from the east.

9. Another view of the main front of the Terminal Station, showing the rich coffering inside the arches.
10. Administration seen from the Basin at dusk. A bandstand flanks it on the immediate left. An electric fountain plays in front. At the far left, one of the rostral columns. At the right, the Columbian Fountain and a tower of Electricity.

11. Another view of Administration, with many of the same elements as in the preceding picture.
12. A night view of Administration at the head of the basin.

COLUMBUS AFTER DISCOVERING
THE NEW WORLD MADE THREE OTHER VOYAGES
OF EXPLORATION AND DIED AT VALLADOLID SPAIN.
MAY 20, 1506.

13

14

13. One of the main entrances to Administration. **14.** Model of one of Karl Bitter's sculptural groups for Administration: *The Glorification of War.*

15

15. The Chicago Day crowd in the Grand Plaza in front of Administration and on the bridge between Machinery and Agriculture. The statues of bison were by Edward Kemeys, the moose by A. Phimister Proctor. **16.** The Columbian Fountain, from the south. In the background: left, main entrance to Electricity; right, Manufactures.

16

17. A rendering of Jules-Alexis Coutan's monumental fountain at the Paris Exposition of 1889.

whose sculptures were already beginning to adorn Manhattan and Brooklyn during the years in which the fair was a-building (elements of the Soldiers and Sailors Memorial Arch, 1892; statue of Nathan Hale, 1893); he had already assisted his famous teacher on a Lincoln Park fountain. His Exposition masterpiece, called the Columbian Fountain, but referred to even more frequently as the MacMonnies Fountain, represented the female figure Columbia riding on a barge—with Fame at the prow and Time at the stern—that was rowed by allegories of the arts, sciences and industries; many marine creatures adorned the fountain area. MacMonnies, working on this commission in Paris, based his figure of Columbia on a sculpture that had won him a Beaux-Arts studio prize in 1885.

One of the most amazing publicity statements in Exposition literature was the one claiming that the Columbian fountain "closely resembles a symbolic design said to have been sketched by Columbus." It was actually much more similar to the chief monumental fountain at the 1889 Paris fair, the work of Jules-Alexis Coutan (Fig. 17), whose later sculptural group *Transportation* on New York's Grand Central Terminal has been called the greatest piece of architectural sculpture in America. Coutan's 1889 fountain was described as follows in a contemporary source: "The vessel of the city of Paris cuts through the waves, bearing France, who illuminates the world with her torch and is surrounded by Science, Industry, Agriculture and Art. A figure of the Republic in the stern handles the rudder. The composition is completed by large mermaids that rise from the mass of water, marine genii blowing their horns and children bearing horns of plenty." One French visitor to Chicago also noted a resemblance between the Columbian Fountain and one in Toulon.

At the other end of the Basin was the tallest piece of sculpture on the grounds and one of the fair's main emblems, the gilt 65-foot-high *Republic* by Daniel Chester French (sometimes referred to as *Liberty;* Figs. 19–21). French had been a noted American sculptor since his *Minute Man* of 1873–75, and had already done much architectural sculpture in Saint Louis, Philadelphia and Boston. His many New York pieces include the *Alma Mater* at Columbia University (1903) and the statues outside the old Customs House (1907 ff.) His best-known work is the statue of Lincoln in the Lincoln Memorial in Washington. Other sculptural decoration around the Basin at the fair included a number of rostral columns decorated with ship's prows (ancient Roman trophies for naval victories) and topped with statues of Neptune by Johannes Gelert.

Here and there in the Court of Honor area—on bridges, in front of buildings—were sculptures, chiefly of animals native to the United States, by A. Phimister Proctor, by Edward Kemeys (author of the Chicago Art Institute lions and *The Still Hunt* in Central Park) and by French in collaboration with the noted animalist Edward Clark Potter, whose long career of lion modeling culminated in the supercilious beasts outside the New York Public Library.

The east end of the Basin was closed by the Peristyle complex (Figs. 20–26). An earlier plan (though later than the one for the Venetian Village) had envisioned a semicircle of 13 isolated columns (for the original colonies) at this spot. The name of peristyle, appropriate for this abandoned idea, clung to Atwood's $300,000 rectilinear double colonnade (150 feet high; 830 feet long including pavilions). The Peristyle had a statue-lined roof promenade (sculptor: Theodore Baur), was flanked by identical pavilions, and was pierced in the center by an opening called the Water Gate, which had sculptures by Bela Pratt. This central opening was glorified by a triumphal arch topped with the Quadriga, a representation of Co-

The following two spreads: **18.** The Basin and the Court of Honor, looking east from the Grand Plaza. In the foreground, the two electric fountains flank the Columbian Fountain. Buildings seen from left to right are Manufactures; the Peristyle complex with the statue of the Republic in front of its main arch; and Agriculture. **19.** The reverse view: Agriculture, Machinery, Administration, Electricity and Manufactures seen from behind the statue of the Republic.

20

20. The east half of the Basin, with the Music Hall, *Republic* and Peristyle. The two small circular "Temples of Vesta" nestle in front of the Peristyle ends. **21.** Looking north from the east end of the Basin. Between Manufactures (left) and the Music Hall can be seen (left to right) some of the foreign government buildings (far distance), the Walter Baker pavilion (bisected in the photo by a rostral column) and the model of the warship *Illinois*.

21

22. The central arch of the Peristyle, with the Quadriga. 23. The south half of the Peristyle promenade, with the Quadriga.

24. Visitors resting in front of the Peristyle.

lumbus in a Roman triumphal chariot (the human figures by French; the horses by Potter).

The pavilion at the north end of the Peristyle, the Music Hall, was the Exposition's concert hall for classical music, with 2,000 seats. The south pavilion, the Casino (like its mate, three stories high and 246 by 140 feet in plan), was conceived as a waiting hall for boat passengers. From it there extended into the lake the 250-foot-wide and 2,400-foot-long Pier, which featured a "movable sidewalk," a covered, electrically driven moving belt with passenger benches that ran, for a nickel, from the boat landing out in the lake all the way to the Casino—when it did run, which was not until well into the fair and only intermittently thereafter. It was probably just as well that the planners had abandoned their notion of placing several "movable sidewalks" within the grounds in imitation of the 1889 Paris fair. Earlier plans called for gigantic towers at the lake end of the Pier.

Near each of the "elbows" formed by the Music Hall and Casino stood a small circular "Temple of Vesta"; one of these was the commercial pavilion of a chocolate company.

Flanking the entire south side of the Basin was one of the most aggressively Roman structures of the fair, McKim, Mead and White's Agricultural Building (frontispiece, Figs. 3 and 27–35). It covered an area of 500 by 800 feet and cost $563,840. Inside, two naves of equal width crossed in the center, forming four long courts with three two-story-high aisles in each.

The exterior, with its repeated groups of three bays of

standard width, was enlivened by end pavilions with domes that rose to 96 feet. The large central dome, reaching 130 feet from the ground, capped an inner rotunda that represented a "Temple of Ceres," into which the visitor entered from an elaborate porch in the center of the facade. This porch, with exterior pediment (*The Triumph of Ceres*) by Larkin G. Mead (a brother of McKim's partner, Mead represented at the fair the older generation of American sculptors who had gone to Italy to study before Paris became more fashionable), also featured much other statuary as well as Pompeian-style murals by George W. Maynard.

Crowning the central Agriculture dome was the only statue at the fair by Augustus Saint-Gaudens, who had not originally intended to be personally represented at all. This was the first *Diana*, an 18½-foot-high copper nude done in 1891 as a huge weathervane for Madison Square Garden. It proved too large for that location, came to the Exposition, and was replaced in New York in 1893 by the 13-foot-high version now in the Philadelphia Museum of Art. Philip Martiny, an Alsatian-born sculptor and assistant to Saint-Gaudens, was responsible for much of the other roof-level statuary. His globe-bearing figures of the races of man on each of the corner pavilions reminded French visitors forcibly of Jean-Baptiste Carpeaux's fountain in the Luxembourg Gardens representing the parts of the world; they also resembled statuary on the Rapp gate of the Paris 1889 fair.

The interior of Agriculture was like that of nineteenth-century exposition buildings in general, inasmuch as the

25. The Music Hall. **26.** The Casino, twin sister to the Music Hall.

27

28

29

30

27. Agriculture, seen across the Basin from the southeast corner of Electricity. The Casino is at the far left, the Colonnade at the right. The bear on the bridge was by Edward Kemeys. 28. Agriculture seen from behind a Grand Plaza bandstand surrounded by Chicago Day crowds. Left to right: Peristyle, Casino, Agriculture, a bit of the windmill display to the south, Colonnade, Machinery. 29. A head-on view of part of the Agriculture facade, with a corner pavilion. 30. Agriculture: the central portico and dome, topped by Saint-Gaudens' *Diana*.

31

32

33

34

31. Agriculture: the pediment of the central portico. 32.
Agriculture: looking upward inside the central portico.
33. Interior view of Agriculture. 34. Another angle on the
preceding view.

displays were housed in many separate, freely imagina-
tive pavilions, pagodas and kiosks supplied by the individual exhibitors, whether foreign nations, states of the
Union, private firms or other organizations. Inside Agriculture, foodstuffs were the chief items to be seen, with
special sections for wool, beekeeping, dairying and brew-
ing. In one corner there was a model experimental farm
station. (The 300-by-500-foot annex to the building
housed agricultural machinery.) Some of the exhibitors
gave out free food samples, which made the building
popular at lunchtime.

Abundantly praised for its external glories, Agriculture
was nevertheless the object of numerous complaints. It
was said to be crowded and jumbled inside, with nearly
half the interior space given over to aisles and passages.
Even the directors of the fair had to admit later on that
the roofing was faulty. Not only did the skylights leak;
they were too large, and the upper story became too hot
as the summer progressed. When the glass was painted
dark and curtains were hung just below it, the ground
floor became too dark. (Incidentally, a number of the Exposition interiors featured translucent hangings beneath
the skylights "in combinations of tints varied to suit the
especial conditions of each building.")

Between Agriculture and the Palace of Mechanic Arts
(Machinery Hall) stretched the South Canal, flanked at
its south end by Peabody and Stearns's Colonnade con-
necting the two buildings (the Bostonians also executed
the 60-foot-high Obelisk in the Canal, an imitation of
New York's "Cleopatra's Needle.") The Colonnade complex, which also served as an entrance to the livestock
area, included an 800-seat Assembly Hall for the use of
the Agriculture, Stock and Forestry Departments. The
sculpture atop the Colonnade was by M. A. Waagen. A
General Electric searchlight was also located there (see
Figs. 36–40).

Machinery Hall, by Peabody and Stearns (Figs. 41 &
42), cost $893,090 and covered an area of 846 by 492 feet
(with a foundry annex 490 by 500, and a powerhouse 100
by 1,000). Structurally, Machinery consisted of three
parallel train sheds, each 130 feet wide with a 100-foot-
high barrel roof (it was the planners' intention to sell the
material for actual train sheds after the fair). A 130-foot-
wide central transept pierced all three shed-naves. The
colonnades of the outer cladding resembled those of the
Place de la Concorde buildings in Paris and Perrault's
east elevation of the Louvre. The corner pavilions were
50 feet square. There was a liberal sprinkling of small
domes; the sets of high twin towers were Spanish-influ-
enced (everything Spanish at the fair was in Columbus'
honor). The Victories placed on the pinnacles and other
sculptures were by M. A. Waagen and Robert Kraus.
There were gilt inscriptions on the building, and "strong
colors" were used on the porch ceilings.

The exhibits in Machinery were all devoted to steam
power. The heavy machines stood on the ground floor;

35. The northwest corner of Agriculture at night, with the
General Electric searchlight beaming from the Colonnade.

36

37

38

36. The east bank of the South Canal: Agriculture, the Colonnade with an Intramural Railway station, the Obelisk. **37.** The south end of the South Canal. **38.** The main arch of the Colonnade. **39.** The west bank of the South Canal. Behind the Obelisk is Machinery, with the Administration dome peeping over its northeast corner. Electricity is in the right background.

39

the galleries were for offices, dining areas and toilets. A special feature inside each nave was a traveler crane that had been used in constructing the building and was now adapted with a platform to give visitors rides.

The Mines and Mining Building, which stood opposite the west end of Machinery and had one front on the Lagoon (Figs. 43–47), was by Solon S. Beman (1853–1914), a Chicago architect responsible for that city's Pullman, Studebaker and Fine Arts Buildings and Grand Central Station, not to mention important work in Saint Paul, Omaha and Milwaukee. His work on entire communities included Ivorydale near Cincinnati and the company town Pullman City just south of Chicago (now within the city limits), focus of the bitter Pullman strike in the year that followed the fair.

Mining, which cost $256,447, was 700 by 350 feet in area. Like Electricity, it was the first building in a general international exposition solely devoted to that specific field. Structurally, it was essentially an extensive open space, with a largely glazed roof supported by steel cantilever trusses that formed a clerestory. Inside, there was a system of two-story-high aisles 60 feet wide. The 20-foot-wide central "street" of the interior was called Bullion Boulevard. To the left and right of each entrance were staircases to the galleries.

Not many kind words were expended on the Mining Building's "early Italian Renaissance" exterior imbued with a "French spirit." Van Brunt explained that its massiveness corresponded suitably to the coarseness of the ores and other materials displayed within. The south entrance had sculptural decoration by Richard W. Bock, a local artist who later worked for Sullivan and Wright. Inside, the raw materials and heavy machinery were on the ground floor; the scientific and metallurgical displays were in the galleries. One of the chief attractions was located in Montana's exhibit: a solid-silver statue of Justice modeled after Ada Rehan, the popular star of Augustin Daly's New York stock company.

Alongside Mining, and with a corner on the Basin, stood Van Brunt and Howe's Electricity Building ($432,675; 265,200 square feet; Figs 43, 44, 48–51), roughly in the style of French Renaissance châteaux, but with somewhat capricious open turrets (in an early drawing they appear as onion domes) and with a huge hemicycle for its main (south) entrance. The pediment of this hemicycle was by the above-mentioned Bock (who also designed the Schlitz pavilion in the Manufactures Building); some of the sculptured figures on it were by Hermon Atkins MacNeil, later one of America's most celebrated sculptors. The hemicycle was also the most colorful part of the structure, with pale blue and yellow used on it; the pilasters were painted like scagliola and their capitals painted like bronze. Within this entranceway stood a statue of Benjamin Franklin and his kite by

40. The South Canal flanked by the Machinery portico (left) and by Agriculture. Across the bridges lies the North Canal, with Manufactures extending along its east bank, and beyond. In the far distance can be seen buildings from the north end of the Lagoon.

32 MACHINERY HALL

42

41. Machinery, with its northeast corner in the center of the photo. **42.** Inside Machinery Hall. **43.** Administration viewed from the north (from the Wooded Island), with the north ends of Electricity (left) and Mining (right). **44.** Looking down the north ends of Mining and Electricity to the west entrance of Manufactures. The bridge to the Wooded Island is at the left.

43

44

45
46

45. The north front of Mining. **46.** Inside the Mines and Mining Building. **47.** Mining: Montana's solid-silver statue of Justice.

The Court of Honor and Its Buildings 43

48

48. Electricity, with its southeast corner in the center of the photo. **49.** Inside Electricity, with the Tower of Light in the center. **50.** Another angle on the Tower of Light. **51.** Electricity: Inside the Egyptian Temple of the Western Electric display.

49

46   *The Court of Honor and Its Buildings*

the Danish-born sculptor Carl Rohl-Smith, whose statue commemorating the Fort Dearborn massacre is now in the Chicago Historical Society. Van Brunt felt that the outer styling of Electricity could afford to be more "joyous" than the more severely classic Court of Honor buildings because it was at one remove from the Basin. The high, pitched-roof nave and transept with their clerestories, the skylights and the great extent of window space gave the interior plenty of light.

The exhibits were almost all by American firms; otherwise, only German and French companies were significantly represented. Electricity was conceivably the most interesting building as far as its contents went. Westinghouse's exhibit included numerous inventions by its Croatian-born genius Nikola Tesla, father of much progress in dynamos, alternating current and other fundamental inventions in electricity. The Western Electric Company had three displays, of which one was in the form of an Egyptian temple, mysteriously lighted within. General Electric featured a tower of incandescent bulbs.

American Bell Telephone offered long-distance calls to the East (the first public demonstration of a New York-to-Chicago call had been made on October 29, 1892, eight days after the fair's dedication; the first Boston-to-Chicago call was on February 7, 1893). Phones were also hooked up to phonographs, and to concert halls and opera houses in the East.

Gray's telautograph was an invention that electrically reproduced handwriting at a distance. According to one source, there was also a model household with every conceivable appliance run by electricity.

Edison displayed his latest phonographs, including an instrument that could play a whole opera, one act per cylinder. But the prize Edison exhibit, first shown at the Exposition, was the Kinetoscope, a peepshow machine that ran very short motion pictures on celluloid film. (Doubt has been cast on the reports of its actual presence at the fair, but these reports are quite numerous and circumstantial.) Edison had specifically built his famous Black Maria studio in New Jersey in December 1892 and January 1893 because his old 1889 "photograph building" on the site was no longer large enough to make all the films he expected to show at the fair. Eventually, he dragged his feet on the Exposition preparations for the Kinetoscope, so that there was probably only one of the machines there (hooked up to a phonograph for "synchronized" sound), and the Kinetoscope did not make the stir it deserved until a parlor was opened on Broadway in New York the following April.*

Closing the ring on the Court of Honor and the Basin, we finally come to George B. Post's mammoth Manufactures and Liberal Arts Building, advertised as the largest

*The exposition devoted to electricity (not a general world's fair) at Frankfurt am Main in 1891 is said to have already included the Nuremberg searchlights (to be described) and the electrified household.

52. Manufactures dominates the right side of this view of the west end of the Basin. In the distance, past the long west side of the building, can be seen the domes of Fine Arts and Fisheries.

53

53. This statue of a black carter, by Daniel C. French (horse by Edward C. Potter) stood in front of the south facade of Manufactures. In the background, Machinery and Administration. **54.** The southwest corner of Manufactures at the south end of the North Canal. The polar bear on the bridge was by A. Phimister Proctor. In the distance, to the right of Manufactures: the Peristyle with Quadriga, the *Republic*, Agriculture.

54

55. The southeast corner of the Manufactures roof promenade, with a German searchlight. Seen below, left to right: Agriculture, the Colonnade, the South Canal with Obelisk, Machinery, the Columbian Fountain, Administration. **56.** Another view from the Manufactures promenade. From left to right: Machinery, Administration (with the Columbian Fountain in front of it and the Terminal Station behind it), Electricity.

57

57. The west side of Manufactures along the North Canal. Domes in the distance include Illinois, the Marine Café, Fine Arts and a lateral pavilion of Fisheries. **58.** The west entrance to Manufactures. The pumas were by Kemeys.

58

59. The east (Lake Michigan) front of Manufactures, with the Viking Ship in the foreground, and the very Dutch little pavilion of Van Houten & Zoon cocoa snuggled near the northeast corner of the giant building.

building in the world (Figs. 52–61). It was 1,687 by 787 feet in area and cost $1,837,601. Its semicircular, glazed, sea-green main roof was 245½ feet high. The corner pavilions (triumphal arches with single openings) rose 97 feet; the four center-of-facade pavilions (triple-opening arches), 132 feet. Of the standard 20-odd-foot bays, there were 22 on the north and south facades, 58 on the east and west! The Corinthian regularity of the facades was partially enlivened by numerous female figures.

Originally, Manufactures was to have consisted of two parallel "tunnels" connected by intersecting ones at either end, and spanned in the center by a depressed dome. Two six-acre courts were to have been left open within the area. De Young, the above-mentioned California member of the National Commission, urged that these courts be roofed over and that one vast central hall be spanned by steel trusses. The celebrated Galerie des Machines at the 1889 Paris fair was the model for this; in an explicit spirit of rivalry, Post's building beat Dutert and Contamin's by a few feet with its 368-foot clear-span hinged-arch roof structure, but the metal detailing on the French edifice was decidedly more elegant and graceful.

Inside, Manufactures had a gallery 50 feet wide, and 86 smaller galleries for viewing that projected 12 feet. Extensive mural decoration included work by such eminent painters as Gari Melchers, Walter McEwen, J. Alden Weir, Robert Reid, E. E. Simmons, Kenyon Cox, J. Carroll Beckwith, Walter Shirlaw, C. S. Reinhart and Edwin H. Blashfield, most of whom would in a few years be

decorating the Library of Congress, an important permanent showcase for White City ideals.

On the main floor of Manufactures were many national pavilions (with individual firms represented within) displaying such stylish manufactured products as ceramics, metalwork, textiles, furniture, glassware and jewelry. Germany's exhibit had a wrought-iron gateway made by Armbruester Brothers of Frankfurt am Main. These gates were purchased after the fair for $20,000 by the owner of the mansion at 1000 Lake Shore Drive (built by Beman in the 1880s). In 1897 this became the honeymoon home of Harold and Edith Rockefeller McCormick, whose stormy marriage and intimate patronage of the arts and sciences were to supply newspaper copy for decades.

The main thoroughfare inside Manufactures, 50 feet wide, was called Columbia Avenue. At its center was the 120-foot-high clock tower of the American Self-Winding Clock Company. At the north end of the Avenue was the giant telescope that Yerkes had ordered for the University of Chicago observatory that was to bear his name.

The galleries of Manufactures were reserved for the Liberal Arts displays (physical development, medical apparatus, education, literature, public works, research instruments, government, commerce, institutions of knowledge, social associations, religious associations, music and theater). Many universities and publishing houses had important exhibits here; photography was not neglected. Musical instruments, alone of all Liberal Arts items, were shown on the main floor of Manufactures. The anthropology and ethnology division of the Liberal Arts Department had its own building elsewhere, as did the Manufactures division devoted to shoes and leather (similarly, the forestry division and the main dairy division were not in the Agricultural Building).

The roof promenade of Manufactures (reached by elevator for 25 cents) provided the best views of the Exposition until it was closed after the disastrous Cold Storage Fire on July 10. On this roof level were several powerful navy searchlights (one source says only one) by Schubert & Co. of Nuremberg, an important feature of the fair at night that recalled the powerful lights beamed from the Eiffel Tower in 1889.

A row of small commercial buildings lined the east front of Manufactures along the lake, with two chocolate-company pavilions at the ends. At the north was the Van Houten pavilion by G. Weymann of Holland. At the south was the festive Walter Baker & Co. pavilion, interesting as being the only work at the fair by the up-and-coming New York firm of (John M.) Carrère and (Thomas) Hastings, who had already made a mark with luxury hotels in Saint Augustine, Florida; who would conceive the major plan for the Buffalo fair in 1901; and who would bestow upon New York City such imposing White City-style landmarks as the Manhattan Bridge entrance and the New York Public Library.

(The Viking Ship seen near Manufactures in Fig. 59 arrived in Chicago on July 12, 1893, after sailing across the Atlantic from Bergen, Norway.)

60. The pavilion of Walter Baker & Co., cocoa and chocolate, to the east of the southeast corner of Manufactures. **61.** Inside Manufactures: the wrought-iron gateway to the German exhibit.

4

THE BUILDINGS ON THE LAGOON

The Lagoon, a creation of Olmsted's that still graces Jackson Park, provided the chief north-south axis of the Exposition. Olmsted wanted it to be more spacious, but plans for a branch railway—never built—between the Midway and the Court of Honor prevented this. With the exception of the Palace of Fine Arts, all the main buildings still to be described faced onto the Lagoon. Starting at the southwest corner, not far from the Court of Honor, its attractions will be followed in a clockwise direction. It will be seen that the rigid norms of the Court of Honor did not apply here.

Perhaps no other image of the World's Columbian Exposition has been cherished over the years as warmly as the Transportation Building's Golden Doorway (or Golden Door; it also had other appellations, such as Gate of the Sun). And for a long period in this century, the Transportation Building received the attention and acclaim as a Sullivan masterpiece that are now more readily granted to his Wainwright Building in Saint Louis, his Guaranty Building in Buffalo and the mausoleums on which his gift for lush flat ornament is seen at its most unconfined.

It was not until 1895, two years after the fair, that the brilliant engineer and acoustician Dankmar Adler (1844–1900) left the major Chicago firm of Adler and Sullivan—a departure that apparently impaired the subsequent career of Louis Henri Sullivan (1856–1924). But Adler had virtually no hand in the Transportation Building, its structural parameters having been arranged by the Exposition planners.*

To understand Transportation (Figs. 62–64), it is necessary to consider it along with its one-story, nine-acre annex, in which many trains were displayed. This annex abutted the main building on the west and opened into it, providing long vistas; the 32-foot bay modules of the main building were based on the width of two pairs of the rails that were laid down on the annex ground. Aside from this, the building was structurally of a rather plain basilica plan (a Roman architectural type),† with the higher central nave furnishing a clerestory and the

*Adler and Sullivan had refused to build a concert hall for the fair.
†Frank Lloyd Wright, an assistant of Sullivan's up to the Exposition period, later reported that everything about Transportation other than the doorway had given Sullivan much trouble.

62. Transportation. At the far left, Mining; far right, the Choral Building.

63. Approaching the Golden Doorway of Transportation. 64. The Golden Doorway. 65. Choral Building, also called Festival Hall. 66. Band concert inside the Choral Building.

67

67. Horticulture, seen across the Wooded Island. At the far left, the Choral Building (with the Ferris Wheel above it on the distant Midway). At the right, the principal structures seen are the White Star pavilion, the Woman's Building and the California state building. **68.** The central block of Horticulture.

68

69. The main entrance to Horticulture, with the two sculptural groups by Lorado Taft. **70.** Inside the Horticulture dome: the artificial mountain and the mammoth Crystal Cave. The latter was one of the few attractions not on the Midway that required an additional admission fee.

71. Looking south along the west bank of the Lagoon. Left to right: Transportation, Horticulture, White Star, Puck, Children's, Woman's.

whole topped with a lookout cupola rising to 165 feet above the ground, and reached by eight elevators (within a cylindrical core) for 10 cents a ride. The area of the main building was 960 feet by 256 feet; its cost, $312,324.

The most startling thing about the exterior, of course, was its polychromatic boldness. The base was a light, delicate red, and there were about 30 other shades, chiefly reds, oranges and yellows, so that the building could be amicably termed "autumnal." The Golden Doorway appeared more like green and silver to careful observers. Its receding arches were related to those on many other Richardson-inspired Sullivan buildings, but here were incredibly ornate. Its ribbons contained quotations by Bacon and Macaulay (not yet present in very early photographs). Angels appeared all along the arcade. Many sculptures were provided by John J. Boyle, an uninspired graduate of the Ecole des Beaux-Arts.

Inside, the prevailing color was dull ochre. A 72-foot-wide gallery was reached by six elevators. Normal for the era, and especially appropriate for the matchless rail center Chicago, was the dominance of trains among the exhibits. Famous locomotives of the past on display included the *Pioneer* of 1833, which had first run between Chicago and Galena in 1848; the 1831 *DeWitt Clinton* of the Mohawk and Hudson line; and the *Lord of the Isles* of

Britain's Great Western Railway, which had been shown when new at the Crystal Palace in 1851.

The Transportation Building has had a mixed press in its own day and at the present time. In 1893, a public-relations officer of the fair wrote that "every nook, nave, corridor and grand gallery is built for a purpose" and that Transportation possessed this merit "more than any building in Jackson Park." On the other hand, Van Brunt, who had to describe the Exposition buildings dutifully for publication, only barely concealed his distaste for Transportation beneath circumlocutions and ironies. The critic Gustav Kobbé found the angels hilarious, and wondered whether their presence on a transportation building was symbolic of the many fatal accidents caused by the public conveyances of the time, the victims of which were then "transported" to a better world.

Since the close of the above-mentioned period of axiomatic adulation, recent critics have called Transportation bad as an exhibition hall, pointing out that it made no creative use of the marvelous nineteenth-century precedents in metal-and-glass construction. It has been demonstrated that Sullivan himself was eclectically applying historical ornament just as freely as the White City architects, except that his was Islamic and Byzantine rather than classical. Finally, it has been made clear that the French awards Sullivan received for Transportation were for its ornament, not for its architecture. Older critics had written that Transportation manifested "a new

ornamental style developed from geometric and plant forms" and had anticipated Art Nouveau by some years, but more recent writers trace Sullivan's ornament to mid-Victorian style books.

As with some other Exposition departments, there was not enough room for all exhibitors within the Transportation Building; the New York Central and the Pennsylvania Railroads had their own smaller structures.

Next to Transportation stood the building designed for more popular concerts, the 6,500-seat Choral Building, or Festival Hall (Figs. 65 & 66). Completed in the last days before opening, it was designed by Francis M. Whitehouse of Chicago, who was to have designed the Venetian Village and—some say—the Palace of Fine Arts.

The Horticultural Building (Figs. 67–70), essentially a huge greenhouse or conservatory, was by the firm of (William Le Baron) Jenney (1832–1907) and (William B.) Mundie (1863–1939). Jenney was the great engineering genius (in the Civil War he had served as Army engineer with Grant and Sherman) whose two Leiter Buildings, two Home Insurance Buildings and other achievements in Chicago make him for many the father of the steel-frame skyscraper.

Horticulture consisted of four long one-story galleries or "curtains" (two front and two rear), with two-story pavilions at the north and south ends of the building, and a central pavilion capped with a glass dome 187 feet in diameter and rising 113 feet from the ground. The

historical cladding was "Venetian Renaissance" and based on elements of Sansovino's Library of Saint Mark. Flanking the main entrance were two sculptural groups by Lorado Taft of Chicago,* *The Sleep of the Flowers* and *The Awakening of the Flowers*. Various shades of green were used on the ornamental ironwork of the exterior. The area of the building was 998 by about 250 feet; the cost, $268,850.

Inside, the two front "curtains" had glass roofs and were devoted to floriculture. The two rear "curtains," only partially glazed above, were for fruit exhibits. Of the two courts between the front and rear "curtains," one contained a grove of lemon and orange trees, and the other contained aquatic plants and a German wine cellar. The pavilion at the south end was dedicated to viticulture; that at the north, to canned goods, seeds and vegetables. Under the central dome was an artificial mountain covered with vegetation, beneath which was a replica of South Dakota's Mammoth Crystal Cave (10 cents admission).

Outside the building were auxiliary greenhouses. Flowers were also displayed on lawns and on the Wooded Island in the center of the Lagoon.

At the northeast corner of Horticulture was the freestanding circular pavilion of the White Star Steamship Company (the firm that owned the *Majestic* and the

---

*Taft, an eminent sculptor who taught at the Art Institute, later wrote a standard history of American sculpture.

72

73

72. The White Star Steamship Company pavilion. To the right of it, the Puck Building. In the far distance at the left, the towers of Electricity and the Administration dome. **73.** Puck Building. **74.** Children's Building. **75.** Woman's Building, with its southeast corner in the center of the photo.

COPYRIGHTED 1893 BY C.D.ARNOLD.

Teutonic), ocular proof that McKim, Mead and White could unbend from the severely classical when the opportunity offered (Fig. 72). The pavilion represented the pilot house of an ocean steamer, the "piazza" (veranda) being the promenade deck. It is interesting to note that at Paris in 1889 the Compagnie Générale Transatlantique, the main French steamship line, had had its own circular pavilion with a veranda. (The C.G.T. dioramas of 1889 were exhibited in Sullivan's Transportation Building in 1893.)

Just to the west of the White Star pavilion, McKim, Mead and White struck again with the Puck Building (Fig. 73). This jolly pink-and-white confection housed the temporary Exposition branch of the famed New York magazine of political cartooning and satire. Visitors could view the latest five-color presses and other marvels of printing technology in operation. The statue of Puck was by Henry Baerer, sculptor of some Central Park and Prospect Park statuary. Supervising the Chicago operation was the founder and chief caricaturist of the magazine, Viennese-born Joseph Keppler. Apparently the unwonted problems at the fair put an excessive strain on Keppler; he left Chicago a very sick man and did not live through the following winter.

To the west of Puck—and protected, as it were, by the Woman's Building, of which it was a dependency—stood the Children's Building, by the French architect Alexandre Sandier (Fig. 74). Inside were a gymnasium, day

76. The east (Lagoon) front of the Woman's Building, with the Ferris Wheel in the distance. **77.** Mary Cassatt's mural in the Woman's Building. **78.** The central figures in Mary Cassatt's mural.

nurseries and many instructional exhibits on child raising that elevated the Exposition's Children's Building far above its Paris 1889 counterpart, which had been dubbed a "hatcheck for babies."

One of the most distinctive features of the World's Columbian Exposition was the Woman's Building (Figs. 75–78). There had been a separate women's pavilion at the Philadelphia Centennial in 1876 and at the New Orleans Cotton Centenary of 1884, but they could not begin to compare in significance with Chicago's contribution to feminism.

This was no accident. At an earlier period in Chicago's history, the brides that successful but lonely businessmen "imported" from previously settled districts of the United States had done much to bring culture to the rough young city. After the Civil War, society had blossomed out and the clubwoman tradition remained very strong. It remained strong not only for amusement but also in the interests of community service, and of women's rights in particular. Queen of Chicago society at the time of the Exposition, and guiding spirit of the Woman's Department and Building, was Bertha Honoré Palmer, a Chicagoan of Kentucky patrician stock, and wife of Potter Palmer, the merchant and hotelkeeper

79

80

79. The Wooded Island and Lagoon from the Manufactures roof. The most prominent structures, left to right: the northeast tip of Horticulture; Puck and White Star; Woman's; the Bureau of Public Comfort with California looming behind it; Illinois of the lofty dome; tiny Merchant Tailors; a Fisheries pavilion; and a slice of the U.S. Government Building. **80.** A view similar to the preceding. Here, the bareness of the trees allows a good look at the Japanese Ho-o-den on the Wooded Island. Just beyond the Fisheries pavilion is the Marine Café. **81.** Illinois Building, with the Merchant Tailors Building in front of it to the right.

The Buildings on the Lagoon 65

82

83

82. Merchant Tailors Building: a gondola on the Acropolis. **83.** Marine Café.

84. Fisheries Building. **85.** The main entrance to Fisheries.

extraordinary who developed State Street commercially and was the first to build a mansion on the Near North Side.

Chicago was also associated with such strongminded and progressive women as Jane Addams, Harriet Monroe, the Temperance crusader Frances Willard and the great champion of women's rights Susan B. Anthony. Susan B. Anthony played a large role in planning the Exposition's Woman's Department – but behind the scenes, to avoid frightening the sedate.

At first, the Woman's Department, run by the Board of Lady Managers, had only minor functions, such as appointing jurors for various Exposition areas in which women were traditionally competent; but eventually the Woman's Building represented a duplicate fair within the fair – not competitive (for awards, etc.) with other areas – in which it was shown that women were capable in just about every department except such strenuous ones as heavy machinery, mining and the like.

The Woman's Building was the only one at the fair for which an architectural competition was held. The winner, who received $1,000, was Sophia G. Hayden, a young graduate of the Massachusetts Institute of Technology. The building was more or less an Italian Renaissance villa with a two-story great hall onto which rooms of varied shapes and uses opened. Its area was 199 by 388 feet, and it cost $140,168. The statues that crowned it were by young Alice Rideout of San Francisco. At the dedication ceremonies of the building, a *Jubilate* by Mrs. H. H. A. Beach was performed.

Some of the exhibits inside were a model hospital and model kitchen, but artistic products of the world's women predominated. The north and south tympana of the great hall (too lofty for comfortable viewing from below) contained large, bold murals, about 15 by 72 feet in area. One, by Mary Fairchild MacMonnies (wife of the sculptor and pupil of Puvis de Chavannes), represented "Primitive Woman" (cavewomen were depicted as helpmates to their rugged menfolk). The other mural, "Modern Woman," by Mary Cassatt, the American Impressionist expatriate in Paris, is to modern eyes far and away the most important painting commissioned for the fair. In its left-hand panel, girls were seen pursuing fame; the right-hand panel represented women in the arts (dancing, making music); in the center, women were seen picking the fruits of Knowledge and Science. All the figures wore contemporary dress.

Mary Cassatt was greatly discouraged while painting this mural in Paris. Francis D. Millet, the Exposition's Director of Decoration, was apparently a niggardly employer. Not only was the mural (now lost) little appreciated in Chicago; even the artist's friend and colleague Camille Pissarro was lukewarm. On October 2, 1892, he wrote to his son Lucien: "I wish you could have heard the conversation I had with Degas on what is known as 'decoration' [and on Cassatt's mural in particular]. I am wholly of his opinion; for him it is an ornament that

86. Looking through the Fisheries porch southward to the U.S. Government Building.

The Buildings on the Lagoon 69

87. The east side of the Lagoon. Left to right: Illinois, Brazil, Marine Café, Fisheries, U.S. Government (in front of it, the Ho-o-den on the Wooded Island), Manufactures. At the right: White Star, Puck, Electricity in the distance. **88.** The north end of the Wooded Island with the Ho-o-den. Left to right: Merchant Tailors, Brazil, Marine Café, main portion of Fisheries, eastern Fisheries pavilion, U.S. Government.

should be made with a view to its place in an ensemble, it requires the collaboration of architect and painter. The decorative picture is an absurdity, a picture complete in itself is not a decoration."

As host state of the Exposition, Illinois had a building that stood rather apart from the rest of the state structures—at the north end of the Lagoon, and at the head of several grand vistas—and was willfully grandiose (Fig. 81). But almost no one had a good word for it. The Eastern architects were dismayed by it (partly because its dome was recklessly higher than their norms had allowed), and Sullivan recalled it in 1924 as "a lewd exhibit of drooling imbecility and political debauchery." It cost about $250,000. It had no exterior sculpture. Its architect was Boyington & Co. of Chicago.

S. S. Beman's Mines and Mining Building was for some an example of how the Eastern classical ideals could be botched in clumsy Western hands, but these critics over-

89

looked his tiny Merchant Tailors Building (55 feet square; near the Illinois Building), which was based closely on the beautiful Ionic structures on the Acropolis (Fig. 82). Inside were eight frescos depicting the evolution of clothing. Beman adapted this building design for his First Church of Christ, Scientist in Chicago, which became a model for Christian Science churches throughout the country.

The cheerful "French Gothic" Marine Café (Fig. 83), which stood near the Fisheries Building, specialized in seafood, not yet common fare in the Midwest. It was one of the numerous Exposition buildings by Henry Ives Cobb (1859–1931), important Richardson-inspired architect, author of the master plan of the fledgling University of Chicago campus and executor of such other major commissions as Potter Palmer's famous 1884 mansion on the not-yet-fashionable North Side.*

Cobb's only Exposition structure for one of the main departments was the $216,333 Fisheries Building (Figs. 84–86), which stood on an islet described in 1893 as "banana-shaped"; hence its unusual ground plan. The main building was connected to two pavilions by curved galleries. These circular pavilions had annular inner spaces; one was devoted to angling, the other was an aquarium for which the salt water came from the United States Fish Commission's Woods Hole station in Massachusetts. The aquarium had an ingenious system of illu-

*Cobb is represented in New York City by the 1909 Liberty Tower building at Liberty and Nassau Streets, now (1979) being converted into cooperative apartments.

89. Looking southward down the east bank of the Lagoon. Left to right: Merchant Tailors, western Fisheries pavilion, U.S., Manufactures. In the far distance: Agriculture, Colonnade with Obelisk, Machinery. **90.** U.S. Government Building. **91.** U.S., Manufactures, Ho-o-den.

mination; the light shining through the tanks from an invisible source made it seem as if the viewer were himself underwater.

The main building, 365 by 165 feet in area, had in the center of each long side a 102-foot-long entrance porch projecting 41 feet and flanked with circular towers. Towers, turrets and arcades were liberally used all over Fisheries, which, only hollowly "festive" for some critics, was for others the swan song of the Romanesque Revival. This was not, however, Richardson's massive brown Romanesque, but a merry Mediterranean Romanesque, with blue Spanish glazed tiles on the high-pitched roofs (no second story was needed, so there was plenty of height available for the roofing) and with playful marine decoration on columns and capitals. According to one anecdote, Joseph Richter of Chicago, who executed the porch columns, failed to bring the ornament down to the base because he followed too literally the indications on the preliminary drawings.

The United States Government Building (Fig. 90) was as severely and universally criticized as the Illinois Building, and was held up as a pernicious example of bureaucratic architecture. (The specific culprit in this case was Willoughby J. Edbrooke, the official Treasury Depart-

92. The Ho-o-den.

ment supervising architect; the earliest plans were by his predecessor, James Hamilton Windrim.)* Many features of the exterior, such as the roofs on the corner pavilions, do seem to have been hangovers from the Second Empire style, now anathema to the White City group. Early drawings of the Exposition show a completely different central dome. The building was 345 by 415 feet in area, and cost about $400,000.

The exterior window bays corresponded to the arrangement of columns inside. Nonstructural partitions were used in the interior, which had seven parallel long aisles 50 feet wide. The inner decoration was in the hands of Emil Phillipson. "Roman" red was used on the ground floor, with gold accents. Colors inside the dome included blue, yellow and olive.

Besides the numerous displays by federal departments and bureaus inside the building, the United States exhibits at the fair included, outdoors nearby, a signal-corps display, a weather bureau, an Army hospital, parade grounds, a life-saving station, a naval observatory, a lighthouse display and a full-size working model of the warship *Illinois* (the real ship could not have been moored in such shallow water). The *Illinois* model was a reminder of the growth of the U.S. Navy, which in the late 1880s and early 1890s had moved from twelfth to third place in the world.

Closing off the Lagoon at the southeast was the

*Edbrooke, who had worked in Chicago, is best known for his Romanesque Revival post office building of 1899 on Pennsylvania Avenue in Washington. Before the Exposition he collaborated on civic projects in Atlanta with Franklin P. Burnham, architect of the Cold Storage Building.

Manufactures Building, which has already been described.

In the Lagoon was the Wooded Island. Olmsted had originally wanted no buildings on the Island, but, although it remained chiefly reserved for plantings, a few structures eventually rose on it. Principal among these—and intended as a permanent gift from Japan to the city of Chicago—was the complex of pavilions known as the Ho-o-den, built on the spot by Japanese workmen (Fig. 92). Descriptions of these Japanese buildings contemporary with the Exposition abound in confusion and errors. The three Ho-o-den pavilions were said to be based on various Japanese buildings, including some not at all like them. It seems fairly safe to say, however, that one main inspiration was the Hōōdō (Phoenix Hall) of the Byōdōin monastery at Uji, built in 1053. The original of this masterpiece of the Fujiwara period (897–1185) was often altered subsequently, but was restored to its pristine state in the 1950s.

The Ho-o-den was the first real introduction of Japanese architecture to the Midwest (possibly to the United States as a whole). Ridiculed by some Exposition writers, it is said to have been admired by all the young Chicago progressive architects, of whom Frank Lloyd Wright was *primus inter pares*. It is now a commonplace to compare Wright's prairie-house style with Japanese building traditions: wide roof, horizontal window band, intimate relationship to surrounding nature, flexibility of interior arrangement, uncluttered look, and so on. There can be little doubt that he saw the three-dimensional real thing first at the World's Columbian Exposition.

5

NORTH POND; SOUTH POND; MIDWAY PLAISANCE

The next Exposition sector to be considered is the entire area of Jackson Park north of the Lagoon. Starting with the Palace of Fine Arts, mirrored in the North Pond, the tour will move counterclockwise through the national and state government buildings.

The North Pond (like the north end of the Lagoon) was the home of numerous white ducks. The birds were expected by the authorities to keep the area clean, but some visitors found that they did the opposite.

The most northerly outpost of classicism was also one of its strongest bastions: Atwood's Fine Arts, last of the major fair buildings remaining to be described (Figs. 4 & 93–96). Fine Arts was considered to be particularly pure in its classicism, since many facade elements, including caryatid porches, were closely imitated from Acropolis buildings. Of course, to Sullivan in 1924, this meant that, among the Exposition structures, Fine Arts was "the most vitriolic of them all—the most impudently thievish." Perhaps Sullivan was also recalling the assertion that Atwood had lifted his main entrance, the south portico, from an 1867 drawing that had won the French Beaux-Arts student Henri Benard a Prix de Rome; Benard is reported to have visited the Exposition and good-naturedly admired the execution of his 26-year-old design.

Since Fine Arts was to house art treasures from all over the world, it was placed on a rather isolated site, and more permanent building materials, such as brick (and no wood), were used in its construction, although its facade was of staff like those of the other major buildings. Its cost was $541,795. The 320-by-500-foot main block of Fine Arts (there were also two 120-by-200-foot annex wings) had a simple nave-and-transept plan (each 100 feet wide and 70 feet high), with a low dome (60 feet in diameter, rising to 125 feet from the ground) above the crossing. Early in the fair, the dome was crowned with a figure of Victory, which was later removed. Inside, the long courts formed by the major arteries had side doors that led to 24 picture galleries 30 by 60 feet in area and 30 feet high. No light was admitted from outside. Exterior decorative sculpture was by Philip Martiny, who also worked on Agriculture, and Olin Levi Warner, who had also designed the Exposition 50-cent piece (in addition, Warner had done the facade sculpture for Post's Long Island Historical Society building). The lions flanking the Fine Arts entrance were by Theodore Baur and A. Phimister Proctor.

The works of art exhibited were more varied and adventurous than might be imagined, given the academic leanings of the time. Of course, such notorious members of the French Académie as Bouguereau, Meissonier, Detaille and Gérôme were represented, but also the more delicate Maurice Boutet de Monvel—none of the famous French Impressionists, however. England sent works by Watts, Leighton, Brangwyn, Crane, Millais and Alma-Tadema, among many others. Russia was better represented than at previous world's fairs, and so Americans had their first chance to see oils by Repin, Korovin and Leonid Pasternak (father of poet Boris); in general, Russia was out to make a good showing in numerous sectors of the Exposition. It was also an unusual treat to see a good number of Scandinavian works, including canvases by the Norwegian Krohg (teacher of Edvard Munch) and the Swede Anders Zorn. Other Continental masters in the Palace of Fine Arts whose names are far from forgotten today were Menzel and Lenbach of Germany, Israëls of Holland, Sorolla of Spain and Boldini of Italy.

The United States was extremely well represented by artists who worked in a wide range of styles (outside the French section, Impressionists had a fighting chance). Of about a thousand American canvases in Fine Arts, about half were lent by artists and collectors in New York. The famous American painters with works on display included James A. McN. Whistler, John Singer Sargent, Thomas Eakins, Childe Hassam, William Merritt Chase, Winslow Homer, George Inness, Eastman Johnson and Kenyon Cox. Among the sculptors were Gutzon Borglum, Alexander Stirling Calder, Paul Bartlett and Daniel Chester French. The latter, who had supplied so much of the special Exposition sculpture, was represented in Fine Arts by his important work *The Angel of Death and the Young Sculptor*. There were drawings by Charles Dana Gibson, A. B. Frost, F. W. Kemble, Joseph Pennell, Howard Pyle and Frederic Remington.

The Museum of Comparative Sculpture in the Trocadéro in Paris had sent numerous models and replicas of old architectural ensembles.

Moving along to the separate structures built by foreign governments, we find that architectural fantasy was allowed full rein. Some of these buildings, such as England's Victoria House, were rarely, if ever, open to the public but served as clubhouses for national dignitaries. (Some of the original Jackson Park trees still stood

93. The Palace of Fine Arts on the North Pond. **94.** Main entrance to Fine Arts. **95.** Inside Fine Arts: below the main dome.

in this northeast part of the grounds.)

Brazil's building (Fig. 97), in a "French Renaissance" style, was designed by Colonel Francisco de Souza Aguiar, and cost $90,000.

The Turkish Building (Fig. 98), although built by a Chicagoan, J. A. Thain (who also built the Turkish Village on the Midway), was based very loosely on a fountain constructed for Ahmed III in Istanbul in 1728. Rare woods were used in its construction. It has been stated that the flat, overhanging roof of this Exposition building, as well as its long horizontal window band – not a feature of the original fountain – was yet another source of inspiration for Frank Lloyd Wright.

The Swedish Building (Fig. 99), designed in a modified sixteenth-century style by Gustaf Wickman of Stockholm (who specialized in bank buildings at home), was shipped to the fair in parts. It included ornamental work in brick and other materials that bore the names of the respective manufacturers. Out of Sweden's total appropriation for the fair of $100,000, this building cost $40,000.

The Victoria House (Fig. 100), Great Britain's national building, received its name at the Queen's own request. It was designed in a half-hearted half-timbered style by Robert William Edis, who had done many London clubhouses and alterations of royal residences.

The German Building (Fig. 101), which remained standing longest of all the national buildings in this sector of the fair, was designed by the Düsseldorf architect Johannes Radke in a rambling eclectic style reminiscent of Renaissance town halls in Swabia with their accretions from many centuries. Intended to be permanent, it cost $150,000 out of Germany's total appropriation of $750,000.

In general, Germany was the foreign country best represented at the fair, with this building, the Krupp Building, some of the most elaborate exhibits within the main exhibition structures, and some of the best Midway

Overleaf: **96.** Inside Fine Arts, with awning beneath skylight.

97

97. The national building of Brazil. Right: Marine Café. **98.** Turkish Building.

98

99. Swedish Building. To the left of it and behind: Guatemala. To the right of it: India, Germany.
100. Victoria House, the national building of Great Britain.

101

102

103

101. The national building of Germany, with that of Spain to the left. 102. Norwegian Building. 103. French Government Building.

entertainments. This was no accident: Germany wanted business. It was not only that German-Americans formed a large part of the Chicago population. More particularly, Germany had been sorely disappointed by the response to its exhibits at the 1876 Centennial, at which time its manufacturers had emphasized cheap products. And since the Centennial, the militant policies of Bismarck and others had kept Germany from being adequately represented in the intervening world expositions.

The Spanish Building (partial view in Fig. 101) was a close copy of the Silk Exchange (Lonja de la Seda) in Valencia, a building contemporary with Columbus' voyages.

The Norwegian Building (Fig. 102), by W. Hansteen, was based loosely on the famous medieval "stave churches" of the mother country, of which the oldest surviving classic example is that of Borgund, dating from about 1150.

The French Building (Fig. 103), designed in a highly individual French Renaissance style by Henri Motte and Adrien Dubuisson (the latter worked for a mining firm, and did its pavilions for the Paris fairs of 1889 and 1900), stood on a triangular plot 250 by 175 feet in area. It consisted of two pavilions connected by a curved open colonnade forming a promenade gallery. Among the exhib-

its inside were examples of the Sûreté's anthropometric methods devised by Bertillon.

The area reserved for the states of the Union (partial general views in Figs. 104 & 105) was equally free from White City restrictions, and a number of its buildings rejoiced in vernacular styles that Van Brunt had marked for extinction. Here, again, many structures served as state clubhouses as well as for exhibits; many contained women's departments. Critics found the state area crowded and confused, however.

The Iowa Building (Fig. 106), built by the Josselyn & Taylor Co. of Cedar Rapids at a cost of $35,000, was particularly interesting because it incorporated the old pre-fair Jackson Park Pavilion (compare Fig. 1), which was now called the Corn Palace.

Behind the Iowa Building (and partially visible in Fig. 106) rose one of the unlaid ghosts of the Exposition, the unfinished Spectatorium that Jenney and Mundie had begun for the astonishing playwright, inventor and megalomaniac Steele Mackaye. Mackaye had talked the Exposition planners into building this vast theater, which was to portray the story of Columbus in the form of a pageant ("spectatorio") called *The Great Discovery* or *The World Finder*, using such equipment as a sun cylinder, sky cyclorama, moving stages and a "curtain of light." George Pullman had invested $50,000. Mackaye had approached Dvořák, then teaching in New York, to write a score, and the *Symphony from the New World* is traceable to this project.

84 *North Pond; South Pond; Midway Plaisance*

Many Exposition sites were discussed, including a combination with the Terminal Station, but the Spectatorium was eventually begun just outside the northeast corner of Jackson Park. Plans by the commercially minded backers to add restaurants and similar ungodly facilities within the hallowed building raised construction costs; then, with the Panic of 1893, money became very tight. The city of Chicago had pledged a million dollars in April 1893, but conveniently forgot its promise. When work on the Spectatorium was abandoned, some $850,000 had been poured into it. Late in 1893 it was sold as junk for $2,250.

New York State had provided so much of the fair's whiteness that its building simply *had* to represent the White City ideals (Figs. 107–109). Designed by McKim, Mead and White, and decorated by Millet, it cost $77,000. All academic-reaction buildings reminded learned viewers of a whole host of former edifices; the New York State Building was variously described as copying an old New York City mansion of the Van Rensselaers and the Villa Medici in Rome. Its banquet hall, in the center of the second floor, was sumptuously Roman in cream and gold. Millet's ceiling painting depicted Juno (as the Empire State) encouraging the arts and sciences. In theme, composition and technique this work is perfectly representative of the decorative paintings in the Court of Honor buildings. Furnishings for the New York State Building were supplied by such New York City firms as W. & J. Sloane and Duveen Bros. After the fair, the building would have been presented to the Board of Lady Managers as a permanent home for a museum of women's work, but the Chicago's South Park commissioners would not allow this.

West Virginia's Building (Fig. 110), a Colonial residence costing $20,000, was by an architect named Silsbee. The Joint Territorial Building (also in Fig. 110), representing the states-to-be Arizona, Oklahoma and New Mexico, was by Seymour Davis, who also did the Kansas Building.

Very popular with Exposition visitors was Henry Ives Cobb's Indiana Building (Fig. 111), a "French Gothic" mansion that cost $60,000. Its red towers reposed on gray staff walls.

Also "homey" and inviting was the placid Wisconsin Building (Fig. 112), a "modern villa" built by William Waters of Oshkosh for $70,000. Its materials were brown stone from Lake Superior, pressed brick from Menomonie and wooden shingles.

The sprawling California Building (Fig. 113) was based on the Mission architecture of the home state. It was built for $120,000 by A. Page Brown of San Francisco, architect of the Ferry Building in that city. One of the exuberant displays inside was a life-size knight on horseback entirely composed of prunes.

104. A group of state buildings. The most prominent are Texas (left foreground), Kansas (right foreground), New York (two tall square towers), Pennsylvania (imitation of Independence Hall), Kentucky (center of photo) and Missouri (bulbous low dome, right). The main block of Fine Arts rises between Pennsylvania and Missouri.

105

Following are a few more statistics on the state buildings that are visible in Figs. 104 & 105. Texas: by J. R. Gordon of San Antonio; $40,000. Pennsylvania: by Thomas P. Lonsdale of Philadelphia; a replica of Independence Hall; the original Liberty Bell was on display. Kentucky: by Maury & Dodd of Louisville. Missouri: by Gunn & Curtis of Kansas City; $45,000. Maine: by Charles S. Frost (an associate of Cobb's); $20,000. New Hampshire: by G. B. Howe "of Boston and Omaha"; $12,000; it resembled a Swiss chalet because that state is "the Switzerland of America." Connecticut: by Warren R. Briggs of Bridgeport; $12,000. New Jersey: by Charles A. Gifford. Rhode Island: by Stone, Carpenter & Wilson of Providence; $10,000. Massachusetts: by the already familiar Peabody and Stearns; $20,000; a replica of the John Hancock residence.

The sector of the Exposition south of the Court of Honor, including the South Pond, contained such practical dependencies of the Agriculture Department as the cattle pens; a few makeshift structures for exhibits that had been crowded out of the main buildings; and an interesting miscellany.

105. Another group of state buildings. In the left foreground, Iowa. Across the Intramural Railway tracks, Maine, New Hampshire, Connecticut, New Jersey, Rhode Island and Massachusetts stand in front of the east annex of Fine Arts. Layered behind Fine Arts are national government buildings, U.S. and Fisheries, with the gigantic roof of Manufactures in the middle distance and the Administration dome far away. Along the lake shore at the left, the French and German buildings and Victoria House are prominent. **106.** Iowa, with the never-completed Spectatorium behind it. **107.** New York State Building. *Overleaf:* **108.** Detail of the banqueting hall in the New York State Building.

Moored in the South Inlet were models of Columbus' three caravels of 1492, the *Santa María, Niña* and *Pinta.* They had been built at Barcelona and towed across the Atlantic from Cadiz, arriving in Chicago on July 12, 1893, the same day as the Viking Ship.*

Near the caravels, on a raised promontory with a rampart-like wall, was another venture of McKim, Mead and

*The writer has not ascertained whether the *Santa María* replica at the fair was the same as the one said to be moored in a Lincoln Park lake as late as 1926; one of the ships (the same?) was definitely still in the Jackson Park boat harbor in the early 1930s. Technically, the original *Santa María* was not a caravel but a decked ship.

109

109. Vault of the banqueting hall, with painting by Francis D. Millet. 110. West Virginia and the Joint Territorial Building (Arizona, Oklahoma, New Mexico). 111. Indiana Building. 112. Wisconsin Building.

110

113

113. California Building. **114.** South Inlet: the *Santa Maria* alongside the Casino. At the left, the *Republic* and Manufactures are visible.

114

115. Along the southern lakefront. Left to right: a corner of the Shoe and Leather Building, the Krupp exhibit, the tiny Convent of La Rabida, the Casino and Peristyle, and the Pier with the Movable Sidewalk. **116.** Forestry Building.

117

118

White, a replica of the Franciscan monastery Santa María de la Rábida near Palos, where Columbus received shelter and encouragement in 1486. The Exposition "Convent la Rabida" housed Columbus documents and memorabilia of dubious authenticity.

Krupp's Gun Exhibit, supported by the German government as well as by the Essen firm, displayed Krupp's latest and most enormous cannon. The special railroad cars on which the gun was shipped across country from its Baltimore landing place were on display in the Transportation area of the fair. The Krupp Building was by either G. Gillhausen of Essen or H. T. Schmidt of Frankfurt (sources differ).

The Shoe and Leather, Dairy and Anthropological Buildings, thrown up at a late date to house overflows, had no architectural merit, no touch of grace, even though Dairy was by the great classicist Atwood.* Leather was by Sandier, architect of the Children's Building. Anthropological was interesting for its collections, such as Stewart Culin's group of primitive games. Zelia Nuttall, for whom a famous Mexican pictorial codex is named, helped set up the exhibits, and the eminent anthropologist Franz Boas was associated with the Physical Anthropology section.

Also related to the Anthropology division, though in the nature of entertainments, were the ruins of Yucatan and Cliff Dwellers exhibits just outside Anthropological and the Esquimaux Village at the northwest corner of Jackson Park. The cliff dwellers were those from Battle Rock in Colorado.

The Forestry Building (Fig. 116) may also be difficult to associate with Atwood, but he was its designer. Built of various woods, and entirely without metal, in a "rustic order," it was 528 by 208 feet in area and cost $100,000. The veranda columns were tree trunks left in their natural state. The sides were formed of wood slabs with the bark removed. The roof was thatched with tanbark and other barks. The interior was finished in various wood surfacings. The 1889 Paris fair had had an analogous wooden forestry pavilion, but more sophisticated and more like a classic Swiss chalet.

The French Colonies building by the South Pond, near the windmill display (Fig. 117), were other echoes of 1889. The Tonkin structure was the very same one that had been designed in the Far East, reassembled on the Champ de Mars and then sent on a tour of France after the Exposition Universelle.

One of the purely functional structures in the South Pond area, the Stock Pavilion for animal displays just south of the Colonnade between Agriculture and Machinery, was not considered "architecture" at the time of the fair but is quite attractive to modern eyes for its modest but far from clumsy simplicity (Fig. 118). It was the work of the outstanding Chicago partners William Holabird and Martin Roche, who had already done the

*He also did the undistinguished Bureau of Public Comfort Building near the California Building.

117. Along the South Pond: the windmills and the French Colonies. 118. The Stock Pavilion.

steel-frame Tacoma Building and were soon to complete their extension of the Monadnock and their Marquette Building. This exposition arena was 280 by 440 feet and had 15,000 seats. The inward-sloping iron roof that protected the spectators from the sun and rain was supported on slender colonnettes similar to those in traditional Spanish patio architecture. Holabird and Roche also designed the national Exposition building of New South Wales.

For thousands of visitors, the fair meant the Midway. For the fair corporation, the Midway meant solvency. This was the first separate amusement area in a world's fair, and a volume as long as this one could be written about its entertainments alone; but it would be a different sort of volume, offering almost no architectural interest. Most of the Midway exhibits that were not merely temporary shacks were feeble imitations of buildings and places elsewhere. The foreign-village type of show, introduced at the Paris 1889 fair and destined for a long life, was omnipresent in Chicago. Java, Cairo and Algeria-and-Tunis were basically as they had been in Paris; the two separate Irish Villages, on the other hand, were surely a bow to the many local Irish-Americans (see Fig. 120).

It was only to be expected that there would be much fakery on the Midway. For instance, a German visitor found that the girls in the World Congress of Beauty of the International Dress and Costume Company did not know their supposed native languages, but all felt at home in the Viennese dialect. Nevertheless, the folklorist Stewart Culin stated that the fair's chief display of folklore was to be found on the Midway.

Only a few Midway highlights that have some historical or other special interest can be mentioned here. The tour will move west along the 60th Street side and then east along the 59th Street side.

Hagenbeck's Animal Show, staged by the great German zoo director and animal trainer Karl Hagenbeck in a big collapsible steel arena, included lions that rode horses and tigers that rode velocipedes.

The Natatorium became a variety show in the last months of the fair.

The Panorama of the Bernese Alps was a so-called "electric theater" in which light and sound effects, used together with landscape paintings, created the sensation of a mountain storm.

The Ice Railway combined a rink and a toboggan slide.

Just to the north of this, in the center of the Plaisance, stood one of the Exposition's great engineering marvels—a deliberate rival to the 1889 Eiffel Tower—one of its great emblems and one of its lasting gifts to the amusement of mankind: the giant wheel (Figs. 121–123) invented and constructed by the Pittsburgh engineer George W. Ferris, a bridge builder, tester of metal bridge elements, and contractor. Ferris received the go-ahead only in November 1892, but the wheel was ready by late June of 1893.

The 45-foot-long axle of the Ferris Wheel was the largest single piece of steel that had yet been forged. The

96 *North Pond; South Pond; Midway Plaisance*

actual wheel was 250 feet in diameter, but the full height at the top was 264 feet, and riders had a remarkable view of the fair and of nearby parts of Chicago. There were 36 wood-veneered cars with room for 60 people in each, 40 of whom could sit on plush-covered swivel chairs. The 50-cent ride included two revolutions and lasted 20 minutes. Six stops were made per revolution, changing the load of six cars at a time.

The Ferris Wheel's expenses during the fair were about $400,000, its gross $726,805.50, leaving a profit for its backers even after the fair corporation took its prearranged half of the gross above $300,000. After the World's Columbian Exposition, this original wheel was dismantled until 1895. It was then used again in a North Side neighborhood, but business was poor. After service at the Saint Louis fair of 1904, it was scrapped in 1906. There was an imitation of it at the Paris fair of 1900, in which year the famous Viennese counterpart, the Riesenrad, was built in the Prater.

The very popular Old Vienna exhibit (Figs. 124 & 125) was largely a reconstruction of the Viennese street Der Graben as it was supposed to have looked about 1750. One of its exhibits was a valuable group of late Egyptian mummy-case portraits.

The Dahomey Village housed inhabitants of the warlike land subdued with such great difficulty by France just before the fair. One contemporary writer said that bringing Dahomeyans to Chicago would teach them just how overwhelmingly powerful the whites were.

Before leaving the 60th Street side, it should be noted that all along it there stretched a special elevated railway (a dependency of the Transportation Department) with speedy cigar-shaped cars on runners, propelled by turbine motors over a film of water. This type of railway had been shown in Paris in 1889.

On the 59th Street side lay the biggest moneymaker of the Exposition (it had been wildly popular in Paris), A Street in Cairo. Its 1893 site was designed by Henry Ives Cobb. Besides the topographical reconstructions, there were camel and donkey rides, bazaars — and girls who did the *danse du ventre*. The most famous of them was "Little Egypt," whose real name and nationality are given by sources old and new in a bewildering variety of forms. It is with her that we associate a tune that has become part and parcel of the American consciousness, the "hootchy-cootchy" dance:

119. The east half of the Midway seen from the Ferris Wheel. The Woodlawn Avenue viaduct crosses the thoroughfare. Closing the prospect is the Woman's Building. Down the left side, from near to far: A Street in Cairo, the German Village, the Javanese Village. Down the right side, near to far: the Moorish Palace, the Turkish Village, the Panorama of the Bernese Alps, the Natatorium and, farther down, Hagenbeck's Animal Show. Along the far right side: the elevated railroad that ran on a film of water. Exposition landmarks in the distance, left to right: Fine Arts, Illinois, Fisheries, U.S., Manufactures, Horticulture, Electricity, Transportation, Administration.

120

121

120. The Irish Industries show at the southeast corner of the Midway. **121.** At the foot of the Ferris Wheel. **122.** The Ferris Wheel, from the southwest. **123.** Ferris Wheel geometrics.

122

123

100 *North Pond; South Pond; Midway Plaisance*

125

126

124. Entrance to Old Vienna. **125.** The courtyard of the Old Vienna area. **126.** Muybridge's Zoöpraxographical Hall, with a minaret from A Street in Cairo.

Music researchers have not yet turned up the full story of this tune. If it is really Algerian, as bibliographer James Fuld's findings strongly suggest, it may even have been first used on another part of the Midway. There were several Near Eastern theaters with bellydancers, and an 1893 song sheet—earlier than any noted by Fuld*— though not using the tune, speaks of "the naughty girls from Algiers" who "do the 'Kouta Kouta' dance." More work is obviously needed in this area. (Incidentally, as far back as the 1876 Centennial, there had been a scarf dance in a Tunisian café.)

In front of A Street in Cairo (just about where the Exposition map included in this volume shows a Diorama of the Destruction of Pompeii that was apparently never built) stood the little Zoöpraxographical Hall (Fig. 126) in which the extraordinarily inventive English-born photographer Eadweard Muybridge, under the auspices of the U.S. Government Bureau of Education, projected very short action sequences of analysis of motion, selected from his 781 photographic plates of "animal locomotion" published by the University of Pennsylvania in 1887.†

Muybridge's projection device, called the zoögyroscope or zoöpraxiscope, was a cross between a traditional optical toy (like the phenakistoscope) and a magic lantern. He had already been touring with it for a few years. Its design is directly traceable to apparatus that had been used in France—to animate drawings, of course, and not photographs—as early as 1850.

It is interesting to reflect that in two widely separated parts of the fair, relatively small and indifferent audiences were watching two inventions that each contained a germ of the "movies." The Edison Kinetoscope in the Electricity Building was showing brief entertainments on celluloid film (which was flexible enough to allow the showings eventually to grow and grow in length)—but only one person at a time could see them. Muybridge was exhibiting educational subjects that were limited by nature to an extremely brief span—but was projecting them to a (potentially) large audience. The problem that lay ahead for inventors was to combine the best features of the two devices: to project films. This desideratum was achieved simultaneously in several countries within two years after the Chicago fair, and we fortunately possess stirring live-action records of the Paris fair of 1900 and the Pan-American Exposition at Buffalo in 1901.

*"Naughty Doings on the Midway Plaisance," words and music by W. C. Robey, published by Will Rossiter, Chicago. This song appears to invalidate the contention that the hootchy-cootchy was never really danced at the 1893 fair. It has also been denied that "Little Egypt" was ever there; perhaps this only means that the dancer of that name who later appeared in Coney Island was not the same as the one in Chicago.

†Perhaps he was also including some more recent work, since one Exposition source mentions insect motion, which is not a part of the 1887 magnum opus.

6

FROM OPENING TO CLOSING DAY, AND BEYOND

Of course, the Exposition was not just static groups of buildings and exhibits; it was also a series of events. A few of these will be touched on here.

Almost immediately after the fair opened, the Panic of 1893 broke out. This stock-market crash led to one of the worst depressions in American history. In Chicago, unemployment soared during 1893, and the winter following the fair was one of great hardship for many. In 1894, George Pullman's inhumane demands on his all-but-enslaved employees at Pullman City drove them to strike. As their spokesman, the labor organizer Eugene V. Debs came into national prominence. President Cleveland, who had opened the fair with the touch of a button, called out federal troops over the protests of Governor Altgeld of Illinois. This liberal governor had pardoned the imprisoned Haymarket rioters during 1893.

A direct early effect of the Panic on the fair was the failure of the bank that had a branch in the Administration Building, where several foreign visitors had made deposits. A few of the Exposition officials had to dip into their pockets to make good.

The Panic did not materially affect the fair's business, but nevertheless this was unsatisfactory for the first three months, picking up only gradually after the weather improved, unfinished areas were completed, the farmers had gathered and sold their crops, and the railroads had belatedly reduced fares.

Sunday openings, though hotly contended, did not help much. When Congress had made its last appropriation for the Exposition, it had included a no-Sunday clause. Despite outcries of treachery and ungodliness, the fair corporation attempted to overlook this stipulation because Congress had reneged on part of its grant. Eventually the fair was closed on only four Sundays and open on 22, but the severe reduction of facilities on Sundays, combined with the reluctance of the public, made the Lord's Day a money-losing one. But, having fought for the privilege, the directors were forced to keep the fair open on the Sabbath long after they had lost the desire to do so.

Many specific days during the fair were set aside for special celebrations in honor of nations, states, organizations and so on. Parades, athletic contests and other amusements characterized these increasingly frequent occasions, which the more dour condemned as a "Barnumization" of the fair, a commercial scheme to bring Midway-type attractions onto the main part of the grounds. June 15, for example, was German Day, and Carl Schurz made a speech. Chicago Day, October 9, the twenty-second anniversary of the devastating fire, brought the biggest crowds of any single day – well over 700,000 visitors. On Poets' Day, August 30, Otis Skinner and Rose Coghlan performed *As You Like It* in an outdoor setting.

Perhaps the most interesting of these events to Americans today was Colored People's Day, August 25. The Exposition as a whole neglected the contributions of black citizens to American civilization, but on that day, in the Choral Building, Frederick Douglass gave an address on "The Race Problem in America,"* Paul Laurence Dunbar read a poem he had written for the occasion, the Jubilee Singers performed spirituals, and the composer Will Marion Cook – later to write musical-comedy songs for Bert Williams and George Walker – presented selections from his opera *Uncle Tom's Cabin.*

Exposition visitors found plenty of entertainment in Chicago that year outside Jackson Park and the Midway. Just beyond the grounds, on a 14-acre site between 61st and 63rd Streets, where rent was cheaper than on the Midway and admission prices noncompetitive, Buffalo Bill's Wild West Show made even more money than the most lucrative Exposition amusements. Colonel Cody gave 318 performances over a six-month period to audiences averaging 12,000, and made a profit of nearly a million dollars. It was here in 1893 that his show first included the Congress of Rough Riders of the World, named no doubt in homage to the Exposition Congresses. At theaters in Chicago's central business district (the Loop-to-be), Lillian Russell, pride of the Midwest and toast of New York, was appearing in comic opera, and Florenz Ziegfeld, Jr., son of the director of the Chicago Musical College, was presenting the strongman Eugene Sandow. The Kiralfy Brothers' spectacle *America* ran for months at the Auditorium.

*Douglass, who had been America's ambassador to Haiti, also delivered a speech on the dedication day of that nation's Exposition building.

Overleaf: **127.** Jackson Park and the Midway Plaisance in 1936, basically as they are today. Of the grand Exposition buildings, only the Palace of Fine Arts, now the Museum of Science and Industry, remains. The lagoon and island are clearly recognizable, but the area of the old Basin and Court of Honor is greatly altered.

The various Congresses (international conferences or symposiums) associated with the Exposition, and held in the new building of the Art Institute at Michigan and Adams, were the brainchild of Chicago lawyer and educationist Charles Carroll Bonney. There were Congresses on medicine, education, finance, temperance, evolution and art. In the Congress on architecture, important papers by Olmsted, Burnham and Sullivan explained many aspects of the fair. Josiah Royce and John Dewey participated in the Congress on philosophy. Many distinguished women, including Julia Ward Howe, spoke at the Congress of Representative Women, but the best-attended session of that particular Congress was the discussion of woman's place in drama by the great Polish actress Helena Modjeska; the American star of emotional melodrama Clara Morris; Georgia Cayvan,* leading lady of the important Lyceum Theatre stock company in New York; and the still very young Julia Marlowe.

At the Congress on literature there were papers by George Washington Cable, Charles Dudley Warner and Richard Watson Gilder. Richard R. Bowker, editor of *The Publisher's Weekly*, made a speech about the world copyright situation. Perhaps the single most important Exposition Congress paper was delivered at the historians' division of the literature Congress. This was the epoch-making thesis by University of Wisconsin professor Frederick Jackson Turner, "The Significance of the Frontier in American History." This paper, said to have "opened a new period in the interpretation of the history of the United States" (*Dictionary of American Biography*), attempted to show that American democracy was of native frontier growth; in fact, was a product of the old Northwest (by then the Midwest).

Most colorful of the Congresses was that on religions, at which religious leaders from *almost* everywhere (the Archbishop of Canterbury, for one, declined the invitation) expounded the tenets of their respective creeds. Such harmony and understanding reigned that many observers thought the millennium was at hand. An immense personal success was scored by the wildly romantic 30-year-old Hindu sectarian Vivekananda, who "exercised a wonderful influence over his auditors." He stayed on in the United States making converts; this was a period in which foreign mystic religions, and such new twists on familiar religions as Christian Science, appealed increasingly to souls stifled by countinghouse air.

One particularly stirring Congress was much more controversial: the one pertaining to labor. One of its meetings was a mass rally held outdoors on the lakefront on August 30. Among the speakers were Henry George, Samuel Gompers and Clarence Darrow (for whom a bridge in Jackson Park is now named).

Many interesting visitors came to the Exposition that year. Highly honored during the opening days were the Infanta Eulalia of Spain (because of Columbus) and the Duke of Veragua, said to be a direct descendant of the Great Admiral of the Ocean Sea. It is sobering to reflect

that, five years later, their fawning American hosts would destroy what was left of the Spanish Empire, and God would personally instruct President McKinley to annex the Philippines.

Another foreign noble visitor, associated with yet another war that would involve the United States, was Archduke Ferdinand, heir to the throne of the Austro-Hungarian Empire. He did not make himself popular in Chicago.

Many American writers visited the fair and waxed enthusiastic. For the journalist and novelist Richard Harding Davis, the Exposition was "the greatest event in the history of the country since the Civil War." Hamlin Garland's injunction to his parents not to miss the fair has often been quoted. For many years, memories of the fair turned up in real, fantastic or allegorical form in numerous American writings, including Edna Ferber's *Show Boat* and the musical based on it.

One of the greatest American photographers, William Henry Jackson, became associated with the fair. He had a business in Denver at the time and was just visiting when he was asked to help out by producing an official set of pictures for a commissioners' report. He charged his usual fee of $10 each for a hundred 11-by-14-inch negatives, but also sold a duplicate set for another $1,000 to Harry Tammen, a curio-shop owner in Denver, who published them in an 1894 volume called *The White City (As it Was)*. The photographic compositions are admirable, but their reproduction in the book deplorable. In addition, the Baltimore & Ohio Railroad exhibit at the fair used about 100 photos by Jackson, including a 30-foot panorama. His association with the B. & O. then led to an adventurous subsidized trip around the globe with the World's Transportation Commission.

The origin of the turn-of-the-century muckraking movement has also been traced back to a visit to the fair. New York magazine publisher S. S. McClure sent a reporter there to get material on the Armour Institute of Technology. The reporter also sent back interesting copy on everyday life in the meatpacking industry. In 1897, McClure asked Ida Tarbell to do a similar study of the Standard Oil Company, and the rest is history.

It had been intended to close the Exposition in a blaze of glory, but on October 28 Carter Harrison, popular mayor of Chicago, was shot in the doorway of his home by a crazed malcontent, and the closing ceremonies on October 31 were muted. On the last night of the fair, the "rabble" on the Midway became exceptionally boisterous and tried to loot the Chinese Theatre, but this was prevented by the Columbian Guard.

When the fair came to an end, it was disclosed that there had been about 27½ million admissions, only about 6 million having been free. Total expenses amounted to about 30½ million dollars, total receipts to about $32,750,000. The concessions had provided about four million dollars of these receipts—about four times what had been expected—and this made possible a 10-percent dividend to the stockholders.

Fire had been a constant threat to the Exposition. Warnings had been published that the major buildings

---

*Georgia Cayvan had a spun-glass dress made for her at the Libbey Glass Works on the Midway. Later the Infanta Eulalia of Spain followed suit.

were not sufficiently protected by neutral zones. Negligence in construction had claimed the Cold Storage Building on July 10, 1893. Now fire began to strike again and again, perhaps not unassisted by arsonists.

On the evening of January 8, 1894, a blaze broke out in the Casino at the southeast corner of the Court of Honor, spread along the Peristyle and gutted the Music Hall at the other end of that colonnade. Flames leaped over to the Manufactures Building and damaged portions of the roof over the French and Belgian displays. Many valuable exhibits that had not been removed were damaged, including the famous bronze vase by Gustave Doré.

In the last week of February 1894, the Colonnade between Agriculture and Machinery was burned.

On the evening of July 5, 1894, the rest of the Court of Honor buildings went up in smoke. The fire started in the Terminal Station, spread from there to Machinery, then to Administration, then to Electricity, then to Mining, then to Manufactures. This was a severe blow to the Chicago Wrecking and Salvage Company, which had purchased this property for $100,000.

In its issue of October 3, 1896, the *Scientific American* reported that the World's Columbian Exposition Salvage Company had just completed its removal of the other buildings. The Golden Doorway of the Transportation Building was still in Jackson Park, owned by a local dealer in statuary who had offered it to the city of Cleveland for $1,200. The statue of Franklin that had stood in front of Electricity had been purchased by the University of Pennsylvania. (Other fairground statues went to Chicago parks and commercial buildings and to other American cities.) The four lions at the base of the Peabody and Stearns's Obelisk had been put out to pasture at the Elgin, Illinois, farm of Harlow N. Higinbotham, former President of the Exposition.

Remaining in Jackson Park in 1896 were the Palace of Fine Arts, which, as the Columbian Museum, then housed the statue of Columbus that had stood in front of Administration and one group of races of man from the Agriculture roof; the German building, in dilapidated condition; the Ho-o-den; the monastery of La Rábida; French's *Republic;* and the whaling bark *Progress* in the South Pond area.

The German Building was eventually rehabilitated (about 1900 it housed a refectory and museum) and adorned the park until it, too, burned in 1925. The Japanese Phoenix Hall on the Wooded Island did not arise refreshed from the flames that consumed it in 1945.*

Luckiest of all the Exposition buildings was the Palace of Fine Arts. As mentioned above, it was converted into an art museum almost immediately after the fair (perhaps it would be more correct to call it an art storehouse at this early period). It remained the Field Colum-

bian Museum until 1920, when it was closed. Then, at the time of the next Chicago world's fair, A Century of Progress, in 1933–34—a fair that shrieked with vivid colors and architectural modernism—this old-fashioned Greek academic building of Atwood's was completely rehabilitated and its facades made permanent, with funds given by Julius Rosenwald, philanthropic head of Sears, Roebuck & Co. It reopened as the Museum of Science and Industry just in time to receive many exhibits from A Century of Progress, and is still going strong today. Beloved of Chicagoans (and a tourist mecca, of course), it offers proof that changing architectural fashions need not destroy public affection for buildings with old and warm associations.

Incidentally, the World's Columbian Exposition received a special homage from the planners of A Century of Progress. The 1933 fair was opened by electric power generated from the light of the star Arcturus, light that had been emitted 40 years earlier, at the time of the 1893 fair.

Jackson Park today (1979) is a pleasant place,* put to good use by neighborhood residents. Its terra firma consists chiefly of lawns, playing fields and a vast golf course; its chief curse is the heavy traffic that zooms along its many car lanes. Along the lake are a few small sandy areas, chief of which is the Jackson Park bathing beach with its long pavilion. The other post-fair buildings are merely nondescript service structures. The topography of the park is generally as Olmsted created it, except in the southeast, where the old Basin is no more and there are now two equivalents of the South Pond, used as marinas. The old North Inlet is a marina devoted to angling for and snagging Lake Michigan salmon.

The area north of the Museum of Science and Industry is at present just a parking lot for the museum. The public entrance of Atwood's sedate-looking old building is now on the north side of the main structure. "Future shock" (for someone immersed in the 1893 fair) begins immediately upon stepping inside, because in the 1930s the buildings received a thoroughly Modern Style, or Art Deco, vestibule. On passing beyond the vestibule, there are no longer any terms of comparison. The building is one huge scientific penny arcade in which learning is made easy and instantaneous by a constant assault on all the senses. The only slight nod that has been made to the original structure and plan of the building is the placement of a large circular model of the periodic table of the elements directly below the central dome, where a gigantic statue of Washington stood during the 1893 fair.

The promontory on which the sham monastery of La Rabida stood is now an open belvedere, but just to the south of it, where the Krupp cannon was exhibited in 1893, the name of the monastery is enshrined in the La Rabida Children's Hospital, with buildings dated 1931 and 1953.

The Wooded Island is now the Paul H. Douglas Nature Sanctuary, named for the distinguished economist and U.S. Senator from Illinois. Near its north end, where the

---

*In recounting the fate of the various Exposition buildings, mention could also be made of the numerous hotels that had sprung up around Jackson Park to house visitors to the fair. A number of these lingered on for years as cheap apartment buildings. Early in the twentieth century the low red structures at 57th Street and Stony Island Avenue sheltered a colorful colony of Chicago bohemians.

*Much less picturesque is the ride there from the North Side or the Loop, through harrowing sections of the South Side.

Ho-o-den was located, a solitary stone garden lantern of a traditional Japanese type is all but hidden behind trees just off a footpath.

At the corner of Richard and Hayes, the approximate site of the Administration Building, stands a peeling 24-foot-high replica of French's *Republic*, which was unveiled in 1918.*

The Midway Plaisance, so raucous in 1893, is now a noble thoroughfare with several malls, car lanes, and pedestrian walks. Its impressive unbroken length is accented by only three pieces of civic sculpture. Quite near Jackson Park stands an allegorical statue of Czech president Masaryk, depicting him as a medieval warrior. About halfway down the thoroughfare is a straightforward statue of the great Swedish naturalist Linné.

At the extremity of the Midway Plaisance farthest from Jackson Park, where the street comes to an end just inside Washington Park, stands a major work by Lorado Taft, who 29 years earlier had done the entrance sculptures for the 1893 Horticultural Building. (Taft's studio was not far away, at 60th and Ingleside.) This monumental termination of the Midway is the large fountain of brown stone, dedicated in 1922, called *The Fountain of Time*. The figure of Time stands by the rim of the basin near the spectator and looks across the water at a historical procession of mankind playing its brief role and marching toward oblivion.

*The *Republic* also served as a model for the fountain figure in the 1895 Siegel-Cooper department store on lower Sixth Avenue in New York City, the store with the famous slogan "Meet Me at the Fountain."

BIBLIOGRAPHY

The listing includes only items that proved of direct use in the making of this book. Item (11), the standard fairground guidebook, is naturally invaluable. Items (39) and (40) are by far the best statement of the architectural program by a participating architect; item (23) is also important in this respect. Readers especially interested in exhibits at the Exposition will find many pictures of national and company pavilions in (24) and of individual objects in (3). Additional views of the Midway and other entertainments, which are not emphasized in the present book, will be found in most of the old picture books listed. Further details of all kinds are gathered most compactly in (3) and (17). For a clear modern discussion of various architectural trends ca. 1890, the present writer is deeply obligated to (54). Item (44) will surely long remain a basic text on the Chicago and Prairie "schools" of architecture. For items in this list from which pictures are reproduced in the present volume, see "Picture Sources" on page vii.

BOOKS BEFORE 1900

(1) Arnold, C. D., & Higinbotham, H. D., *Official Views of the World's Columbian Exposition*, Department of Photography, World's Columbian Exposition Company, Chicago, 1893.

(2) *Authentic Visitors' Guide to the World's Columbian Exposition and Chicago. . . . Condensed Information Compiled from Official Sources. Revised to Date*, The Union News Company, Chicago & N.Y. [1893].

(3) Bancroft, Hubert Howe, *The Book of the Fair: An Historical and Descriptive Presentation of . . . the Columbian Exposition at Chicago in 1893 . . .*, The Bancroft Company, Chicago & San Francisco (editions in 1, 2 and 10 vols., 1893–95).

(4) Buel, J[ames] W[illiam], *The Magic City / A Massive Portfolio of Original Photographic Views of the Great World's Fair . . .*, Historical Publishing Company, St. Louis & Philadelphia, 1894 (reprint: Arno Press, N.Y., 1974).

(5) Cameron, William E., *The World's Fair, Being a Pictorial History of the Columbian Exposition . . .*, 1893 [no publisher or city; entered for copyright by J. R. Jones].

(6) *The City of Palaces. A Magnificent Showing of the Glories of the World's Fair*, W. B. Conkey Company, Chicago, 1895.

(7) *Columbian Album / Containing Photographic Views of Buildings and Points of Interest about the Grounds of the World's Columbian Exposition*, Parts 2–14, Rand, McNally & Co., Chicago, 1893.

(8) *Columbian Exposition / Dedication Ceremonies / Memorial . . .*, The Metropolitan Art Engraving and Publicity Co., Chicago, 1893. [Also describes events between dedication and opening of the Exposition.]

(9) *Das Columbische Weltausstellungs-Album*, Rand, McNally & Company, Chicago & N.Y., 1893.

(10) Elliott, Maud Howe, *Art and Handicraft in the Woman's Building of the World's Columbian Exposition / Chicago, 1893*, Goupil & Co., Paris, 1893.

(11) Flinn, John J., ed., *Official Guide to the World's Columbian Exposition in the City of Chicago, State of Illinois, May 1 to October 26, 1893, by Authority of the United States of America . . .* (handbook ed.), The Columbian Guide Company, Administration Building, Chicago, 1893.

(12) Fourcaud, L[ouis] de, ed., *Revista de la Exposición Universal de París en 1889*, Montaner y Simón, Barcelona, 1889 (Spanish trans. of *Revue de l'Exposition universelle de 1889*, L. Baschet, Paris, 1889).

(13) Hamilton, W. E., ed., *The Time-Saver. A Book Which Names and Locates / 5,000 Things 5,000 / at the World's Fair That Visitors Should Not Fail to See*, W. E. Hamilton, Chicago [1893].

(14) Handy, Moses P., ed., *The Official Directory of the World's Columbian Exposition May 1st to October 30th, 1893*, W. B. Conkey Company, Chicago, 1893.

(15) Jaffé, Franz, *Die Architektur der Columbischen Welt-Ausstellung zu Chicago 1893. Nach amtlichen Quellen bearbeitet von F. J. . . .*, Verlag von Julius Becker, Berlin, 1895.

(16) Jenks, Tudor, *The Century World's Fair Book for Boys and Girls . . .*, The Century Co., N.Y., 1893.

(17) Johnson, Rossiter, ed., *A History of the World's Columbian Exposition Held in Chicago in 1893 / By Authority of the Board of Directors* (4 vols.), D. Appleton and Company, N.Y., 1897.

(18) Monroe, Harriet, *The Columbian Ode* (souvenir ed. with designs by Will H. Bradley), W. Irving Way & Co., Chicago, 1893.

(19) Northrop, H[enry] D[avenport], *The World's Fair as Seen in One Hundred Days . . .*, National Publishing Co., Philadelphia, 1893.

(20) Norton, Frank H., ed., *Frank Leslie's Historical Register of the United States Centennial Exposition, 1876 . . .*, Frank Leslie's Publishing House, N.Y., 1877.

(21) *Official Views of the World's Columbian Exposition Issued by the Department of Photography / C. D. Arnold / H. D. Higinbotham / Official Photographers / 1893 / Press,* Chicago Photo-Gravure Co. [Chicago, 1893].

(22) *Photographs of the World's Fair / An Elaborate Collection of Photographs of the Buildings, Grounds and Exhibits of the World's Columbian Exposition . . . ,* J. A. Hill & Company, N.Y. [© 1894].

(23) *Proceedings of the Twenty-Seventh Annual Convention / American Institute of Architects / Held at Chicago, July 31 and August 1, 1893 // Supplement / World's Congress of Architects,* Inland Architect Press, Chicago, 1893 (papers by Olmsted, Sullivan *et al.*).

(24) Shepp, James W. & Daniel B., *Shepp's World's Fair Photographed,* Globe Bible Publishing Co., Chicago, 1893.

(25) Truman, Ben C. (*et al.*), *History of the World's Fair / Being a Complete and Authentic Description of the Columbian Exposition From Its Inception,* Mammoth Publishing Co., Philadelphia, 1893 (reprint: Arno Press, N.Y., 1976).

(26) Walton, William, *World's Columbian Exposition MDCCCXCIII Art and Architecture,* George Barrie, Philadelphia, 1893.

(27) White, Trumbull, & Igleheart, William, *The World's Columbian Exposition, Chicago, 1893,* P. W. Ziegler & Co., Philadelphia & St. Louis [1893].

(28) Wood, Stanley, *The White City (As it Was),* The White City Art Company, Chicago & Denver, 1894 (photos by William Henry Jackson).

(29) *World's Fair Chicago 1893 Souvenir Illustrated / Being a complete and concise history of the principal World's Fairs . . . ,* The Anabogue Publishing Company, Chicago [© 1891].

(30) *World's Fairs from London 1851 to Chicago 1893 . . . ,* Midway Publishing Company, 1892.

PERIODICALS BEFORE 1900

(31) Adams, John Coleman, "What a Great City Might Be – A Lesson from the White City," *The New England Magazine,* N.S., XIV, 1, March 1896, 3-13.

(32) Cortissoz, Royal, "Color in the Court of Honor at the Fair," *The Century Magazine,* XLVI, 3, July 1893, 323-334.

(33) *Die Gartenlaube* (weekly), Leipzig (several articles by N. v. Stetten and by Rudolf Cronau in 1892 and 1893 issues).

(34) *Harper's Weekly,* N.Y. (dozens of articles and illustrations, 1891-1894; consult magazine's indexes).

(35) Kobbé, Gustav, "Sights at the Fair," *The Century Magazine,* XLVI, 5, Sept. 1893, 643-655.

(36) Levasseur, Emile, "L'Exposition de Chicago. Coup d'oeil sur l'ensemble de l'exposition" (lecture given on Jan. 21, 1894), offprint from the *Annales du Conservatoire des Art et Métiers,* Gauthier-Villars et Fils, Paris, 189-.

(37) Millet, F[rancis] D., "The Decoration of the Exposition," *Scribner's Magazine,* XII, 6, Dec. 1892, 692-709.

(38) *Scientific American,* N.Y. (numerous articles, 1891-1893, including weekly columns during run of Exposition); of particular importance is the article on the fate of the buildings in the issue of Oct. 3, 1896, p. 267.

(39) Van Brunt, Henry, "Architecture at the World's Fair," *The Century Magazine,* XLIV, 1 ff.: May 1892, 81-99; July 1892, 385-399; Aug. 1892, 540-548; Sept. 1892, 720-731; Oct. 1892, 897-907.

(40) Van Brunt, Henry, "The Columbian Exposition and American Civilization," *The American Monthly,* LXXI, #427, May 1893, 577-588.

TWENTIETH-CENTURY BOOKS

(41) Burchard, John, & Bush-Brown, Albert, *The Architecture of America: A Social and Cultural History,* Little, Brown and Company, Boston, 1961.

(42) Burg, David F., *Chicago's White City of 1893,* The University Press of Kentucky, Lexington, 1976.

(43) Carman, Harry J.; Syrett, Harold C.; & Wishy, Bernard W., *A History of the American People* (revised ed.), Alfred A. Knopf, N.Y., 1961.

(44) Condit, Carl W., *The Chicago School of Architecture: A History of Commercial and Public Building in the Chicago Area, 1875-1925,* The University of Chicago Press, Chicago, 1964.

(45) Dedmon, Emmett, *Fabulous Chicago,* Random House, N.Y., 1953.

(46) Fillitz, Hermann, *Das Mittelalter I* (Vol. 5 of *Propyläen Kunstgeschichte),* Propyläen Verlag, Berlin, 1969.

(47) Fontein, Jan, & Hempel, Rose, *China • Korea • Japan* (Vol. 17 of *Propyläen Kunstgeschichte),* Propyläen Verlag, Berlin, 1968.

(48) Fried, Frederick (text), & Gillon, Edmund V., Jr. (photos), *New York Civic Sculpture: A Pictorial Guide,* Dover Publications, Inc., N.Y., 1976.

(49) Fuld, James J., *The Book of World-Famous Music / Classical, Popular and Folk* (revised ed.), Crown Publishers, Inc., N.Y., 1971.

(50) Hamlin, Talbot Faulkner, *The American Spirit in Architecture* (in the series *The Pageant of America),* with foreword by Ralph H. Gabriel, Yale University Press, New Haven, 1926.

(51) Hendricks, Gordon, *The Kinetoscope / America's First Commercially Successful Motion Picture Exhibitor,* The Beginnings of the American Film, N.Y., 1966.

(52) Hitchcock, Henry-Russell, *Architecture: Nineteenth and Twentieth Centuries* (in the series *Pelican History of Art),* Penguin Books, Harmondsworth, 1958.

(53) Jackson, William Henry, *Time Exposure / The Autobiography of . . . ,* G. P. Putnam's Sons, N.Y., 1940.

(54) Jordy, William H., *American Buildings and Their Architects: [Part III] Progressive and Dynamic Ideals at the Turn of the Twentieth Century,* Doubleday, N.Y., 1972 (reprint: Anchor Books, Garden City, 1976).

(55) Kogan, Herman & Rick, *Yesterday's Chicago,* E. A. Seemann Publishing, Inc., Miami, 1976.

(56) Lewis, Lloyd, & Smith, Henry Justin, *Chicago: The History of Its Reputation,* Harcourt Brace and Company, Inc., 1929 (reprint: Blue Ribbon Books, Inc., N.Y., 1933).

(57) Mackaye, Percy, *Epoch: The Life of Steele Mackaye* (2 vols.; esp. II, 311-462), Boni & Liveright, N.Y., 1927.

(58) Mayer, Harold M., & Wade, Richard C., *Chicago: Growth of a Metropolis,* The University of Chicago Press,

Chicago, 1969.

(59) Pierce, Bessie Louise, *A History of Chicago* (3 vols.; esp. Chap. XIV, "The White City," in Vol. III, *The Rise of a Modern City 1871–1893)*, Alfred A. Knopf, N.Y., 1957.

(60) Pissarro, Camille, *Letters to His Son Lucien / Edited with the assistance of L. P. by John Rewald* (trans. from the MS by Lionel Abel), Pantheon Books Inc., N.Y., 1943.

(61) Portoghesi, Paolo, ed., *Dizionario Encicopedico di Architettura e Urbanistica* (6 vols.), Istituto Editoriale Romano, Rome, 1968–69.

(62) Sullivan, Louis H., *The Autobiography of an Idea,* American Institute of Architects, 1924 (reprint: Dover Publications, Inc., N.Y., 1956).

(63) Taft, Lorado, *The History of American Sculpture* (revised ed.), The Macmillan Company, N.Y., 1925.

(64) Tallmadge, Thomas E., *The Story of Architecture in America* (revised ed.), W. W. Norton & Company, Inc., N.Y., 1936.

(65) Tharp, Louise Hall, *Saint-Gaudens and the Gilded Era,* Little, Brown and Company, Boston, 1969.

(66) Thieme, Ulrich, & Becker, Felix, edd., *Allgemeines Lexikon der bildenden Kunstler* (43 vols.), Verlag von Wilhelm Engelmann, Leipzig; E. A. Seemann Verlag, Leipzig, 1907–61.

(67) White, Norval, & Willensky, Eliot, *AIA Guide to New York City* (revised ed.), Collier Books, N.Y., 1978.

PERIODICALS SINCE 1950

(68) Barnes, Sisley, "George Ferris' Wheel: The Great Attraction of the Midway Plaisance," *Chicago History: The Magazine of the Chicago Historical Society,* N.S., VI, 3, Fall 1977, 177–182.

(69) Crook, David H., "Louis Sullivan and the Golden Doorway," *Journal of the Society of Architectural Historians,* XXVI, 4, Dec. 1967, 250–258.

(70) Gebhard, David, "A Note on the Chicago Fair of 1893 and Frank Lloyd Wright," *Journal of the Society of Architectural Historians,* XVIII, 2, May 1959, 63–65.

(71) Hallmark, Donald P., "Richard W. Bock, Sculptor; Part I: The Early Work," *The Prairie School Review,* VIII, 1, first quarter 1971, 5–18; and "Part II: The Mature Collaborations," VIII, 2, second quarter 1971, 5–29.

(72) Hoffmann, Donald, "Clear Span Rivalry: The World's Fairs of 1889 and 1893," *Journal of the Society of Architectural Historians,* XXIX, 1, March 1970, 48–50.

(73) "The Inter-State Exposition Building 1873–1892," *Chicago History,* O.S., VII, 11, Spring 1966, 321–333.

(74) Karlowicz, Titus M., "D. H. Burnham's Role in the Selection of Architects for the World's Columbian Exposition," *Journal of the Society of Architectural Historians,* XXIX, 3, Oct. 1970, 247–254.

(75) Kysela, John D., S.J., "Mary Cassatt's Mystery Mural and the World's Fair of 1893," *The Art Quarterly* (Detroit Institute of Arts), XXIX, 2, 1966, 128–145.

(76) Manson, Grant Carpenter, "Frank Lloyd Wright and the Fair of '93," *The Art Quarterly* (Detroit Institute of Arts), XVI, 2, Summer 1953, 114–123.

(77) Riedy, James L., "Sculpture at the Columbian Exposition," *Chicago History: The Magazine of the Chicago Historical Society,* N.S., IV, 2, Summer 1975, 99–107.

(78) Tselos, Dimitri, "The Chicago Fair and the Myth of the 'Lost Cause,'" *Journal of the Society of Architectural Historians,* XXVI, 4, Dec. 1967, 259–268.

(79) Tunnard, Christopher, "A City Called Beautiful," *Journal of the Society of Architectural Historians,* IX, 1–2, March & May 1950, 31–36.

(80) Weimann, Jeanne Madeline, "A Temple to Woman's Genius: The Woman's Building of 1893," *Chicago History: The Magazine of the Chicago Historical Society,* N.S., VI, 1, Spring 1977, 23–33.

128. Porch with double circular colonnade from an unidentified structure (doubtless a national or state building) close to the Palace of Fine Arts, a facade of which is visible at the right.

INDEX

All references are to pages. An italic number indicates an illustration on that particular page; for double-page picture spreads, only the first page is given. All buildings and other sites are or were located in Chicago unless otherwise stated.